The
Chain
of
Logic

S. Morris Engel

University of Southern California
and Atkinson College/York University

PRENTICE-HALL, INC.
Englewood Cliffs, N.J. 07632

Library of Congress Cataloging-in-Publication Data

Engel, S. Morris, (date)
  The chain of logic.

  Includes index.
    1. Logic.   2. Aristotle—Contributions in logic.
  I. Title.
  BC71.E53   1986   160   86-17058
  ISBN 0-13-124330-6

Editorial/production supervision: Mark Stevens
Cover design: Ben Santora
Manufacturing buyer: Harry P. Baisley

Printed in the United States of America
10   9   8   7   6   5   4   3   2   1

ISBN   0-13-124330-6   01

Prentice-Hall International (UK) Limited, *London*
Prentice-Hall of Australia Pty. Limited, *Sydney*
Prentice-Hall Canada Inc., *Toronto*
Prentice-Hall Hispanoamericana, S.A., *Mexico*
Prentice-Hall of India Private Limited, *New Delhi*
Prentice-Hall of Japan, Inc., *Tokyo*
Prentice-Hall of Southeast Asia Pte. Ltd., *Singapore*
Editora Prentice-Hall do Brasil, Ltda., *Rio de Janeiro*
Whitehall Books Limited, *Wellington, New Zealand*

For my brother
Barney
with love and affection

Contents

Preface

To teach students to be critical, logical, alert, and astute is a goal all teachers share. Most would admit that it is much more difficult than might be expected, and is not always crowned with success. Yet no one is very clear why this is so.

Is it possible that we have turned a basically simple task into an unnecessarily difficult one? After all, isn't a critical person simply one who takes a questioning attitude, who doesn't passively accept whatever is said? And if this is so, aren't there really only two basic questions people need to be trained to ask in order to become critical: Is what has been said really so? and How valid is it?

My own experience has led me to believe that this is indeed so: people need only to be taught to question the truth of statements and the validity of reasoning. It is also clear to me that the task is not easy. For it isn't enough simply to ask ourselves whether the statements offered are true and the reasoning correct. We need to develop a heightened sense of what is relevant to a point in dispute and what our rights are in argument—something that cannot be acquired overnight. It takes time and a good deal of practice to recognize unqualified generalizations, bifurcations, imperfect analogies, and the many sorts of half-truths that pass for evidence. It also takes time and training to recognize what we are obliged to assent to in an argument and what we are justified in rejecting.

I have found that, just as the detailed discussion of the traditional list of fallacies, as first compiled by Aristotle, is excellent training for the first question (that is, Is it really so?), so his treatment of propositions and their various relations and of the syllogism is excellent preparation for the second (Is it valid?). The detailed study of the categorical syllogism leaves us with a deep understanding of and feeling for what is relevant and what constitutes validity. Studying in detail and over some period of time the logical relationship between propositions, and seeing at that basic level what can be said to follow from what and why, imparts an indelible sense of what does and does not constitute adequate support for a given conclusion that can be achieved in no other way.

When I first started to spend a lot of time on the common fallacies some ten or fifteen years ago, I did so because it bothered me that the usual courses in logic did not enable students to recognize such simple things as the fact that just because so many people make use of a certain product (''Gordon's Gin: Largest seller in England, America, the world'') doesn't mean that they should or that it is any good, or that just because a celebrity says he uses a given brand of toothpaste (''If you like people, be sure you brush with Colgate. Walt Frazier wouldn't think of brushing with anything else.'') doesn't mean that he necessarily knows what he is talking about. And even if the students were sufficiently astute to recognize how irrelevant the evidence supporting the conclusions in these appeals or arguments was, were they properly prepared to recognize it in less obvious cases? Could they easily spot it in such examples as ''I fail to see why hunting should be considered cruel when it gives tremendous pleasure to many people and employment to even more?'' or ''If sugar is so fattening, how come so many kids are thin?'' Without some explicit training in identifying types of irrelevance, could they recognize that, while many people find hunting fun, it doesn't mean animals do, or that, although kids are able to stay thin despite the volume of sweets they consume, this doesn't mean that adults can. It became apparent to me that without explicit preparation they simply could not do it, or at least do it very well. And so I began spending more and more time in my logic courses on this topic.

More recently I have come to recognize (along with many other teachers, I am sure) that students are not only unable to tell what is relevant to an argument and what is not, they are not always able to distinguish an argument from a nonargument, or a conclusion from a premise, or tell when a premise provides adequate support for a conclusion and when it fails to do so. In short, before students can recognize cases of irrelevance, they need a clear standard of relevance and validity—a model against which they can then compare examples of faulty reasoning.

And so I have been teaching the study of validity, which trains us to recognize when premises are adequate as support for their conclusions and when they are not, before starting on the study of fallacies, which trains us to recognize ways in which premises may be irrelevant to their conclusions. We also discuss at an early stage the components of arguments.

And indeed I have found that my students are both enlightened and liberated by learning the most basic elements of logical argument: that a proposition consists of a subject and a predicate; that the subject is something about which a statement is made, while the predicate is that which is stated about the subject; that if a proposition lacks one or the other, the person who wrote it may not have been fully aware of what he or she was talking about or intended to say; and that if an argument is unclear, that is a sign of muddle and confusion on the part of the proposer, deserving our scorn and not our assent.

What follows is derived from Aristotle's logical works. These writings, which were given the collective title *Organon* (*Instrument* [of knowledge]) by his successors, consist of six treatises: the *Categories,* which treats of terms; *On Interpretation,* which deals with propositions; *Prior Analytics,* which discusses the doctrine of the syllogism; and the *Posterior Analytics, Topics,* and *Sophistical Refutations,* which deal respectively with scientific, dialectical, and sophistical thinking. Together these works, whose object is to provide us with a standard against which to measure the validity of reasoning, represent the body of classical logic, the oldest humanistic subject in the liberal arts curriculum. This book is intended to be a modern presentation and application, as refined over the centuries, of the first three of these works.

Introduction

Whenever someone gives reasons to support a point of view, that person is offering an argument.

A person's reasons are contained in the *premises* of the argument, and the point of view he or she would like to persuade us of is contained in its *conclusion*.

This raises two basic questions: (1) How good are these reasons? and (2) Do they really lead to the conclusion?

Although one should give one's consent to an argument only after these questions have been answered in the affirmative, this is unfortunately not always the case. We tend to give our consent too readily, only rarely pausing to reflect on the meaning and scope of the conclusion we are agreeing to and to what extent the reasons offered do indeed support it.

Partly this is because we are not often all that clear which is which in a given argument, or sometimes even what is an argument and what merely a statement, a complaint, or an expression of opinion calling for our sympathy rather than our consent. Partly, however, it is also due to our vague perceptions of what our rights in argument are, what it means to logically confirm or prove something, and what this requires. Needless to say, it takes more than merely someone's say-so, even if that someone is a person of eminence.

In what follows we shall learn how to sharpen our ability to distinguish between propositions that assert and those that merely exclaim, between arguments and nonarguments, and between reasons and conclusions. This will enable us to ask in a more meaningful and searching way the two questions we need to ask of every argument.

The first question, concerning the truth of the premises, is a two-pronged one. The premises of an argument may fail to support the conclusion because they are irrelevant to it; on the other hand, such premises may be relevant to the conclusion but inadequate to give it the support it needs. These are two separate problems, and, although there may be some overlapping between the two, it is important to keep them apart for the sake of clarity.

Most advertisements address themselves to almost everything except the question of why *we* should buy the product. They are examples of arguments or appeals whose premises, like those of too many of our current political debates and press conferences, are irrelevant to their conclusions. We are obviously very prone to respond to such irrelevant appeals. To avoid falling victim to them, we must learn to recognize the linguistic ambiguities on which many of them turn, sharpen our skill in detecting the questionable assumptions on which they rest, and develop the insight and muster the courage to resist the biases and prejudices to which they appeal.

There is yet another set of errors against which we must learn to guard ourselves. These are concerned not with the meaning, accuracy, or truth of the premises but rather with what follows from them.

A typical example is the famous aspirin advertisement: ''Bayer is pure aspirin. Bayer is 100% aspirin.'' Can we validly infer from this advertisement, as its sponsors undoubtedly hope we will, that Bayer is the only brand of aspirin that is 100% pure? Can we assume all the others are non-pure? That inference, which goes beyond what is absolutely contained within the given premise, would obviously be invalid. What that premise allows us to infer is that if the tablet in our hand is a Bayer aspirin, then we can be sure it is 100% aspirin—and that is all.

To recognize such traps is to protect ourselves from the designs of advertisers, propagandists, and all those far more interested in their profit than in our welfare. But to do so involves learning to recognize the limits of validity—that is, what it takes to logically prove something.

What the study of logic will teach you is that it takes a lot. This will probably be a sobering discovery, since all our tendencies are to believe just the reverse—and those who pass themselves off as our friends know this about us. To hold these tendencies in check is one of the great benefits to be derived from the study that follows.

ONE

Terms and Propositions

1. THINKING

> Reason is attained by industry, first in apt imposing of names.
> —Thomas Hobbes

If Hobbes is right, it is with "names" that we must begin. What the seventeenth-century English philosopher called "names," however, we now call "words."

We want to understand what it is we do when we think. Thinking, of course, is always about something, and we think about things by fixing them in our minds with words and by combining these words into sentences. To understand thinking, therefore, we need to turn our attention to the identifying labels we attach to things and the manner in which we combine them.

We combine words in all kinds of ways: to make declarative statements ("All men are mortal"), to form questions ("Where are you going?"), to issue commands ("Shut the door!"), and to express our feelings and emotions ("What a play!"). Although each of these is a sentence, only the first is of the type that interests the logician, for only the first can be judged to be either true or false. Combinations of words that can be judged to be true or false are called *propositions* rather than sentences by logicians.

By distinguishing propositions from sentences, logicians mark off for themselves a special area of study—the objective meaning of sentences, not the words that carry such meanings. Of course words are necessary to convey meaning, but what a sentence means is independent of a particular sentence. For the same meaning may be conveyed by other sentences in the same language, and by sentences in different languages. "I came, I saw, I conquered" conveyed the same meaning as "I marched into Gaul, met the enemy, and defeated him" or, as Julius Caesar originally said, "Veni, vidi, vici." It is with the meaning, which remains unchanged, and not the particular words or their grammatical structure, that logic is concerned.

A *proposition* may be defined, therefore, as a sentence that can be said to be true or false. This is the distinguishing feature of propositions. "What a play!" is not a proposition since that remark is not designed to describe what has been observed but rather to express admiration for it. If the speaker had intended it as a description, one to be accepted or debated by others, he or she could have said, using the declarative form, "That was a great play."

2. TYPES OF PROPOSITIONS

There are three types of propositions that logicians have isolated for special study. The first of these, the *categorical proposition,* is simply our ordinary declarative sentence. It has two basic components: a *subject,* about which something is stated, and a *predicate,* that which is stated about the subject. By subject and predicate, logicians mean the complete subject and complete predicate. Since these may consist of several words each (one complete subject, for example, might be "our complicated, technological, and multifaceted culture"), these parts of the categorical proposition traditionally are called *terms* rather than words.

Hypothetical and disjunctive propositions are the other two types the logician studies. A *hypothetical proposition* is composed of two simple categoricals arranged in the form of a conditional, as in "If it rains, then the party will be called off." Although this form is not used as frequently as the simple categorical, we resort to it often in our thinking. A *disjunctive proposition* consists of two categoricals placed in the form of alternatives, as in "Either the man is alive or he is dead." This type of proposition is also not as frequent as the simple categorical, though it is familiar enough.

The study of logic examines all three types of proposition, and all three are important and enter deeply into our thinking. But in what follows we will confine ourselves to the analysis of the categorical proposition—that simple, direct assertion in which something is unconditionally affirmed or denied.

3. THE CLASS ANALYSIS OF THE CATEGORICAL PROPOSITION

When we consider an ordinary proposition like "All roses are red," we are inclined to interpret it as attributing a certain quality to a subject—in this case, that of redness to roses. However, it was part of the genius of Aristotle, who single-handedly founded the science of logic and was the first person to study these matters in detail, to see that the reverse is the case. Far from attributing a certain predicate to a subject, a proposition like this asserts that a certain *subject,* or class of objects, belongs to or is part of a certain other class of objects, or *predicate.* Thus, the proposition "All roses are red" asserts that the class of things called "roses" is part of, or is included in, a larger class of things called "red." This insight into the nature of propositions turned out to be the key to the syllogism, and with it to the nature of thinking.

A class is simply a group or collection of things possessing some characteristic in common. The grouping may be a natural one, as in the group of things called "roses," or it may be arbitrary—for example, "cars with 9,999 miles showing on their odometers". Furthermore, the group may consist of real or imaginary items ("cars," "flying cars"), or of a single member, or none at all ("all those without sin who may cast stones"). Whatever the specific nature of the classes involved, propositions about them assert a relation between classes, one of inclusion or exclusion, either complete or partial.

Let us now look a little more closely at this relation that is so central to propositions.

Every standard categorical proposition has, as Aristotle pointed out, both a *quality* and a *quantity. Quality,* as applied to propositions, refers to whether they are in the affirmative (assert something of something else) or negative (deny something of something else). An *affirmative proposition* asserts the inclusion of one class in another, while a *negative proposition* asserts the exclusion of one class from another. *Quantity* refers to the extent of the inclusion or exclusion— whether it is complete or partial.

In terms of their quality, propositions can therefore be classified as either affirmative or negative. In terms of their quantity, they can be classified as either complete or partial. These four elements in the two classifications—affirmative, negative, whole, part—give rise to four different categorical propositions:

1. A proposition like "All (roses) are (flowers)," in which we are told that all of the first class of things (roses) are included in the second class (flowers).
2. A proposition like "No (Americans) are (illiterate)," in which we are told that all of the first class is excluded from (or not included in) the second.
3. A proposition like "Some (voters) are (wealthy)," in which we are told that some of the first class of things or beings are included in the second.
4. A proposition like "Some (work) is not (ennobling)," in which we are told that some of the first class of things is excluded from the second.

These four propositions have come to acquire two separate sets of names. Propositions that tell us something about all of a class (as in numbers 1 and 2) are called *universal.* Those that tell us something about an indefinite part of a class (as in 3 and 4) are *particular.*[1] The first of the four types illustrated above is

1. *Particular* here means "referring to a part only," an older meaning of the word.

described, therefore, as a *universal affirmative* proposition (universal with respect to its quantity, and affirmative with respect to its quality); the second as *universal negative*; the third as *particular affirmative;* and the fourth as *particular negative.* For the sake of convenience, however, these four forms have come to be referred to by the first four vowels of the alphabet—the first being called an A proposition, the second an E, the third an I, and the fourth an O.[2]

We have noted so far that each of these four types of categorical propositions contains (1) a quantifier (i.e., words such as "all," "no," and "some"); (2) a subject class; and (3) a predicate class. In addition, each contains one further component, traditionally called the "copula." The *copula* is always composed of some form of the verb "to be," such as "is," "is not," "are," or "are not." Its function in propositions is to serve as a link between the subject and the predicate.

Ordinary sentences often lack this rather important element in the proposition. Many examples come to mind: "The good die young," "No cat has nine tails," "Some people live beyond their means." The copula is essential for class analysis, however, and whenever it is missing it must be supplied: "All (those who are good) are (persons who die young)," "No (cat) is (a creature that has nine tails)," "Some (people) are (persons who live beyond their means)." It is worthwhile noting that "is" and "are" are copulas only when they link the subject to the predicate. In the proposition "Workers who are harshly treated are rarely very productive," only the second "are" is the copula; the first is simply part of the subject term.

Some ordinary sentences lack the quantifier, as in the example just given. When this happens, traditional logic assumes that a universal is implied, unless the context makes it quite clear that "some" is intended. Furthermore, the only quantifiers traditional analysis recognizes are "all," "no," and "some," although others ("several," "most," "a few," "the majority," and the like) are in common use. By "all" traditional logic understands "each and every one"; "some" means "at least one and possibly more—perhaps all." We will follow this practice.

Just as quantifiers and copulas must occasionally be supplied, a subject or predicate term sometimes needs to be completed in order to make the original sentence less clumsy in its class-analysis form. In the case of a sentence like "Our opponents are fighting a lost cause," for example, we would change the predicate term to "persons who are fighting a lost cause." In the case of the proposition "Fundamentalists are intolerant of those who disagree with them," we would restate it, "All (persons who are fundamentalists) are (people who are intolerant of those who disagree with them)." Notice that in addition to filling out the subject, we added a quantifier as well.

---

2. The symbols A, E, I, and O were taken from the Latin words *affirmo* (affirm) and *nego* (negate)—the A and I from the former, the E and O from the latter.

These are not the only difficulties we will encounter in translating ordinary propositions into proper class-analysis form. There are several others that will prove more challenging, as we will see. But before turning to them, let us sharpen our understanding of the four types of categorical propositions by noting ways in which they may be symbolized and diagrammed.

4. DIAGRAMMING CATEGORICAL PROPOSITIONS

The universal affirmative (A) proposition asserts, as noted above, that all of the first class of things is to be included in the second class of things. Using the symbols S (for *subject*) and P (for *predicate*), we may represent that proposition symbolically as "All (S) is (P)." Using circles (as first suggested by the eighteenth-century Swiss mathematician and physicist Leonhard Euler), we may represent that same proposition schematically as a smaller circle, S, within a larger one, P.

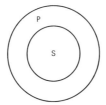

This shows that every S is also a P. The representation also shows that there are P's that are not S's (all those in the larger circle which lie outside the inner one). We will explore later what this implies for what is called the *distribution of terms,* and for reasoning as a whole.

The universal negative (E) proposition asserts, as we saw, that none of the first class of things are included in the second. If we use S for subject and P for predicate, that proposition asserts symbolically, "No (S) is (P)." Using circles, we may represent this same proposition schematically as two separate circles, having no point of contact:

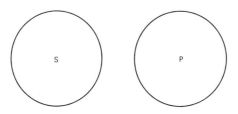

We can see from this representation that these two classes have nothing in common, that they are indeed worlds apart.

The particular affirmative (I) proposition asserts that part of the first class of things is included in the second. Using the symbols S and P, this proposition asserts symbolically, "Some (S) is (P)." We may represent this in diagrammatic form by two intersecting circles, with an X placed in the area where individuals or things are members of both classes:

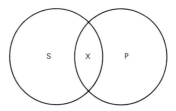

This representation gives us additional information that will be useful to us later. It shows that some P's are also S's, and that there may be S's that are not P's and P's that are not S's.

The particular negative (O) proposition asserts that part of the first class of things is excluded from (or not included in) the second class of things. Using the symbols S and P, this proposition asserts symbolically, "Some (S) is not (P)." We may represent this proposition in diagrammatic form with two intersecting circles, with an X placed in the area where there are S's but not P's:

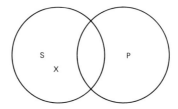

The placement of the X shows us that there are definitely members to be found in this particular area, one where there are no P's. But the proposition doesn't show whether there are any S's in the area where there are P's (that is, where the two circles intersect and individuals are members of both classes).

A good many of these points will emerge again at a later stage in this study, where we will use such diagrams to aid us. Such pictorial devices are useful, for they enable us to see the structure of what is being investigated, not only internally but with our eyes.

5. TRANSLATING ORDINARY PROPOSITIONS INTO CLASS-ANALYSIS FORM

Traditional logic requires that every proposition that isn't expressed in proper class-analysis form be rephrased until it conforms to one of the four basic types. Although such rephrasing can destroy the niceties of expression, we must overlook this in favor of logical accuracy. No logical operation can be performed upon any categorical proposition until it has been put into class-analysis form.

We have already seen that propositions sometimes lack quantifiers and copulas and that their subject and predicate terms may need filling out. Other problems may arise as we translate original sentences into class-analysis form.

Singular propositions pose less of a problem than others. These are propositions that have a single thing or person for their subject: "The table is brown," "John is ill," "Love is blind." For purposes of class analysis, such subjects need to be treated as if they were universal. The justification is simply that when the subject is an individual, we refer to all of it, not just part of it: "All (of the table) is (a thing that is brown)," "All (John) is (one who is ill)," and "All (love) is (a thing that is blind)."

Propositions built around the structure "All . . . is not . . ." or "All . . . are not . . ." are more difficult. Traditional analysis does not recognize their existence, since it operates only with the four types we have discussed above. And it does not recognize such propositions because of their ambiguity. Although in ordinary speech the structure "All . . . is (are) not . . ." is frequently meant to convey a universal negative (E), it could also convey a particular negative (O). If, for example, we were asked "Are all cats black?" we might reply "*All* cats *are not* black," meaning thereby that "Some cats are not black" (O). On the other hand, if we were asked "How many human beings are sinless?" we might reply "All are not sinless" meaning now "No human being is sinless" (E). Close attention to the context should inform us in most cases whether an O or an E is intended (in most cases it will be an O). Therefore, rephrase sentences containing that structure into O forms unless an E form is obviously intended.

Propositions beginning with "Few" and "A few" can also cause problems. The former generally entails an O proposition, while the latter implies an I. Some examples will make this clear. When someone says "Few people saw the accident," the intent is not to assert that there were some people who saw it, but rather to emphasize that many did not. To translate the proposition into an O— "Some (people) are not (those who saw the accident)"—would be more accurate than to translate it into an I. The same applies to such propositions as "Few were saved," "Few can do it right," and "Few survived the crash."

On the other hand, propositions beginning with the words "A few" can be more accurately translated as I propositions. "A few people saw the accident" tells us that some saw it, and hence should be expressed as an I. This is also the case with such examples as "A few were sold," "A few people like it," and "A few made it."

There are other kind of difficulties, however, that will prove more intractable. These concern original sentences whose grammatical structure does not correspond to logical structure.

Unlike many other languages, word relationships in English are not conveyed by inflectional word endings (as was the case even in Old English some nine hundred years ago), but rather by a pattern of word order. In the modern English sentence, this pattern follows logical structure and is the model of simplicity: subject, verb, object. Perhaps because it *is* so simple, however, we have a strong tendency to try to make our speech more interesting by varying and embellishing it in all sorts of ways.

One of the most common of these is the tendency to reverse the order of the subject and predicate. In the beatitude "Blessed are the merciful," the subject is "merciful" not "blessed." In a modern proposition such as "Little has been accomplished by terrorists," the logical subject is "terrorists" and not "persons who have accomplished little." The meaning of this sentence would be distorted if we translated it as "All persons who have accomplished little are terrorists." Obviously, there are other people besides terrorists who may have accomplished little. To put such propositions into proper class-analysis form, we need to reverse the original order of the sentence elements.

There is no simple rule for distinguishing the subject from the predicate. The only suggestion we can make is to place the most favorable interpretation on what has been said and in this spirit restate the original proposition. If it is difficult to make the distinction, this may be a sign that the speaker was not very clear about what he or she was saying.

The case is different with sentences that vary word order with words like "only" or "none but." The speaker's or writer's intent here is clearer, as is our procedure in dealing with it. The first thing to note is that "Only (S) is (P)" or "None but (S) is (P)" are not the same as "All (S) is (P)." "Only women can bear children" is not the same as "All women can bear children"; "None but veterans are eligible for this award" is not the same as "All veterans are eligible for this award." Some women may not be able to have children, and some veterans may not be eligible. Besides, had the speaker intended to say that "All women can bear children" or that "All veterans are eligible for the award," he or she would have said so; in saying that "Only women can bear children" or "None but veterans are eligible for the award," the speaker obviously meant to state more. Thus, we cannot simply drop the "only" in such sentences and replace it with "all."

Propositions beginning with "Only" or "None but," which assert in general that the predicate applies exclusively to the subject named, are called *exclusive propositions*. They can be interpreted as A propositions only when the positions of the subject and predicate are reversed. In translating them, "Only

(S) is (P)'' becomes "All (P) is (S)." The propositions "Only women can bear children" and "None but veterans are eligible for this award" will read "All (those who can bear children) are (women)" and "All (those who are eligible for this award) are (veterans)."

Exclusive propositions also lend themselves to translation into E propositions if the subject term is negated. Another equivalent of "Only (S) is (P)" or "None but (S) is (P)" is "No (non-S) is (P)." Note that in using the E form the terms are not reversed but remain in their original places. The only additional operation (aside from putting it into the form of an E proposition) is to negate the subject term. To use our two former examples, the propositions "Only women can bear children" and "None but veterans are eligible for this award" can correctly be translated into "No (one who is not a woman) is (one who can bear children)" and "No (one who is not a veteran) is (one who is eligible for this award)." It is obvious that these are indeed accurate—and even clearer—translations of the original statements.

We may summarize the rules governing the translation of propositions beginning with "Only" or "None but" as follows:

1. Whenever a sentence is in the form of "Only (S) is (P)" or "None but (S) is (P)," change "Only" or "None but" to "All" and reverse the order of the subject and predicate.
2. Change the "Only" or "None but" to "No" and negate the subject term.

SUMMARY

There are many ways we combine words to form the sentences with which we do our thinking, but only those sentences that assert something about something else (for example, "The grass is green") and can be said to be either true or false are called propositions. Such propositions consist of a *subject* term, a *predicate* term, and a *copula* (a word consisting of some form of the verb "to be") that unites the two. According to traditional analysis, such terms designate *classes* (sets or groups of things having a common characteristic) and each proposition consists of two such classes—a subject class (S) and a predicate class (P)—brought together in specific ways.

There are three main types of propositions: *categorical, hypothetical,* and *disjunctive.* The categorical, unlike the other two, consists of a direct and simple assertion, with no "if" or "or" qualifying it.

Categorical propositions are classified according to their quality and quantity. *Quality* refers to whether a proposition is affirmative or negative; *quantity* refers to whether a proposition includes all members of the subject class or only some. If reference is made to all of the members of the subject class, the proposition is said to be *universal;* if reference is made only to some of the members of the subject class, the proposition is said to be *particular.*

Combining quality with quantity gives rise to four types of propositions: *universal affirmative* ["All (S) is (P)"], *universal negative* ["No (S) is (P)"], *particular affirmative* ["Some (S) is (P)"], and *particular negative* ["Some (S) is not (P)"]. These are usually referred to, using the first four vowels of the alphabet, as A, E, I, and O propositions, respectively.

Many other words besides "some" and "all" are commonly used to indicate how much of a class is referred to in a proposition. Furthermore, ordinary assertions frequently lack copulas, and their subject and predicate terms are often conveyed indirectly. Traditional analysis requires that (for purposes of logical clarity) each proposition be adapted to proper class-analysis form.

When no quantifier is stated, assume that the proposition is universal, unless it is quite clear from the context that "some" is intended. Where the subject term is singular ("Jones," "the table," and so forth), treat it as a universal by expressing it as either an A or an E proposition. Where a subject or predicate is incomplete, fill it out so that it clearly designates a class. In the proposition "Jones is tall," "tall" does not name a collection of individual things; it should therefore be changed to "a person who is tall." And, finally, supply a copula if it has been omitted.

Translate propositions built around the structure "All . . . is (are) not . . ." into either an E or an O proposition, depending upon the context. A proposition beginning with "A few" can be conveyed best with an I proposition, whereas one that begins with "Few" can be expressed as an O. Also remember that what appears to be the subject of a sentence may not be. The subject and predicate may have been reversed for the sake of variety or emphasis. Finally, propositions beginning with "Only" or "None but" can be expressed in proper class-analysis form as either an A proposition (with subject and predicate terms reversed) or an E proposition (with the subject term negated).

Exercises

I. Complete the following statements (See answers in appendix.)

1. A proposition may be defined as a sentence which can be called _____ or _____.

2. Although all propositions are sentences, not all _____ are propositions.

3. The copula is always a form of the verb _____ _____.

4. Words like "all," "none," and "some," which tell us how much or how many of the things designated by the term are being talked about, are called _____.

5. In addition to the simple categorical propositions, logicians are interested in propositions built around the words "if . . .then," which are

called _____ propositions, and those built around the words "either . . . or," called _____ propositions.

6. The four basic types of simple categorical propositions are called

   _____   _____,
   _____   _____,
   _____   _____,
   _____   _____.

7. A proposition is *universal* with respect to quantity if it refers to _____ members of the class designated by the term, and *particular* if it refers only to _____ members of that class.

8. Quality, as applied to propositions, refers to whether propositions are in the _____ or _____; that is, whether they assert or deny something about something else.

9. For the sake of convenience, traditional logic refers to the four types of categorical propositions by the code letters _____, _____, _____, and _____.

10. Traditional logic requires that every proposition not already expressed in class-analysis form be _____.

11. Subjects and predicates in ordinary sentences that do not stand for clear or complete classes need to be filled out by such phrases as "_____," or "_____."

12. When an ordinary sentence omits a quantifier, traditional logic assumes that "_____" or "_____" is implied, unless the context makes it clear that "some" is intended.

13. Propositions that have a single thing or person as their subject are, for purposes of class analysis, treated as if they were

   _____.

14. Traditional logic requires that propositions built around the phrase "all are not" be translated as either a standard E or an O proposition. In the majority of cases these will turn out to be _____ propositions.

15. Propositions beginning with "A few" normally become _____ propositions, while those beginning with "Few" are usually _____ propositions.

16. Propositions beginning with "Only" and "None but" can be better conveyed as A propositions (accomplished by _____ their subject and predicate) or E propositions (accomplished by _____ the subject term).

II. Which of the following are propositions and which are not? Of those that are propositions, label them A, E, I, or O. (See answers in appendix.)

17. What a beautiful day it is!

18. None of these things are easy to do.
19. Please shut the door.
20. Some cars are expensive to keep up.
21. How many are coming to dinner?
22. Some registered voters are not property owners.
23. All seats are gone.
24. If I could only win that race!
25. Do you think you can pass that exam?
26. All of us are students of logic.
27. Have you finished your work?
28. Nobody is here.
29. Stop making that noise.
30. Some people are not trustworthy.
31. Some snarks are boojums.

III. Put the following propositions into their proper class-analysis form by filling out, where necessary, their subject and predicate terms. After bracketing these terms and labelling them with either an S or a P, illustrate each proposition by using circles. The first example has been done.

S   P

32. All crows are black. All (crows) are (black creatures).

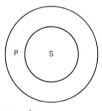

33. Some philosophers are wise.
34. Some people are not lucky.
35. No one is guiltless.
36. All who applied were from out of state.
37. Some players won't make it.
38. Nobody was hurt in the accident.

IV. Restate the following sentences in proper class-analysis form by adding missing copulas, quantifiers, and appropriate additions to subject and predicate terms where needed.

39. No dogs allowed.

40. Universities are complex organizations.
41. Love is blind.
42. Liquor is not permitted on these premises.
43. You can't make fortune smile on you.
44. Rivers flow downhill.
45. Many civilizations have vanished without leaving a trace.
46. Beggars cannot be choosers.
47. Money doesn't grow on trees.
48. You are wrong.
49. Many pleasures are not worth pursuing.
50. Most wounds heal quickly.
51. Blood is thicker than water.
52. Money is the root of all evil.
53. Knowledge is power.
54. Discretion is the better part of valor.
55. Some human beings are never satisfied.
56. Diamonds are forever.
57. Fish live in water.
58. Most pets favor those who feed them.
59. Almost everyone suffers from one guilt or another.
60. Many people lead lives of quiet desperation.
61. Exercise can be hazardous to your health.
62. Spare the rod and spoil the child.
63. They jest at scars who never felt a wound.
64. Persons who are over the age of eighteen can vote.
65. Happy are they who have few wants.
66. He can't be wrong whose life is in the right.
67. Many are called, but few chosen.
68. To meet him is to like him.

V. Do the same with the following sentences, taking account of such expressions as "all are not," "only," "none but," "few," and "a few."

69. All soldiers are not heroes.
70. Only those who enjoy their work are happy.
71. A few students are well off.

72. Only fools will vote for him.
73. Few are they who are both philosophers and kings.
74. None but civilized nations build libraries.
75. Not all Americans pay taxes.
76. None but seniors have been invited.
77. All these children are not of school age.
78. Few dramatists are greater than Shakespeare.
79. Only ignorant people hold such opinions.
80. All the relics from the tomb of Tutankhamen are not precious.
81. A few reflective persons go on to become philosophers.
82. None but the brave deserve the fair.
83. Few streets are safe these days.
84. All sentences are not propositions.
85. Only those in good standing will be considered.
86. All that glitters is not gold.
87. Not all murderers are hanged.
88. Only native-born citizens are eligible to run for President.

TWO

Relations of Propositions

The rules of logic would be easy to apply, and violations easy to detect, if arguments came in neat packages, with premises and conclusions clearly identified and each component in proper class-analysis form. But of course it doesn't work that way. The ordinary argument is clothed in an excess of verbiage, the conclusion is not easily distinguishable from the premises, the language is often confused and confusing, and the whole is often highly repetitive. To deal effectively with such arguments, one first needs to cut away the excess of words and reduce the argument to its bare essentials. Enormously helpful here is the ability to recognize when utterances are logically equivalent and therefore reducible to one another. This is not a talent that can be mastered quickly. It entails a broad knowledge of words and their meanings and an understanding of the ways in which propositions composed of such words may be reduced and related to one another. This chapter is concerned with this task.

Let us begin by noting that two propositions may not be related to each other at all. Such propositions are called *independent propositions*. Being independent, the truth or falsity of one such proposition does not permit any inference to be drawn about the truth or falsity of the other. Knowing that one is true or false, in other words, allows us to draw no conclusion regarding the truth or falsity of the other. ''Universities are complex organizations'' may be true or false, but whatever it is, its truth or falsity tells us nothing regarding the truth or falsity of the proposition ''The brave deserve the fair.'' And this is characteristic of all independent propositions. What makes two such propositions independent of each other is that they have different subject and predicate terms. Both propositions may be true, both may be false, or one may be true and the other false, but knowing what the case is with one allows us to make no inference at all regarding the other.

The situation is different with propositions that contain the same subject and predicate terms. Such propositions are comparable. Although they may differ in quantity (one may be universal, the other particular) and in quality (one may be negative, the other affirmative), the truth or falsity of one stands in direct relationship to that of the other. For example, if it is true that "All men are mortal," then it is also true that "Some men are mortal" and false that "Some men are not mortal." These propositions can be compared with one another because, unlike independent propositions, they share the same subject and predicate terms.

An inference is a conclusion drawn from one or more premises. Where only one premise is involved, as in the example "All men are mortal," the inference is said to be *direct* or *immediate;* that is, the inference can be drawn without the mediation of another premise. Where another premise is involved, as in more complex arguments, the inference is said to be *mediate.* In this chapter we will confine ourselves to immediate inferences.

Knowing what may or may not be validly inferred from a given proposition is useful for two reasons. First, practice in such derivations leads to skill in dealing with the verbiage surrounding ordinary assertions and arguments, enabling one to get to their core more quickly. Second, it serves as a brake against our general tendency to infer more from arguments than is often justified.

The two most basic relations in which two propositions may stand to each other are *conversion* and *obversion.* It is to them that we now turn.

2. CONVERSION

To *convert* a proposition means to interchange the position of the subject and predicate terms. We thereby obtain a new proposition by immediate inference from the given one. This means that if the original proposition is true, the new one derived from it by conversion is true also; and if the original proposition is false, this one is also false.

For example, in the E proposition "No cats are dogs," we are asserting that not a single cat is a member of the class of beings represented by the predicate term "dogs." Now if this is so—if all of the S class is excluded from all of the P class—then we can be sure that the whole of the P class is excluded from the whole of the S class, and that consequently not a single dog is a member of the class of beings represented by the subject class "cats." Any proposition with the same structure as "No cats are dogs" can therefore always be validly converted simply by interchanging its terms. As we will see, this is not the case with all propositions.

It does hold true, however, of the I proposition, which, like the E, is said to "convert simply." Let us consider an example.

A proposition like "Some flowers are now in bloom" asserts that some members of the S class, "flowers," are also members of the P class, "things now in bloom." If it is true that members of these two classes overlap, then it must be true that some of the things now in bloom are flowers. Therefore, I propositions, like E propositions, convert simply. From "Some S is P" we can always validly infer that "Some P is S."

Can we similarly infer from "All S is P" that "All P is S"? From "All ball players exercise daily," can we infer that "All who exercise daily are ball players"? From "All housewives are concerned about inflation," can we infer that "All those who are concerned about inflation are housewives"?

As obvious as it is from these examples that we cannot validly make such inferences, this is a rather common error. In an episode from *Alice in Wonderland,* the Mad Hatter catches Alice making such faulty inferences and urges her to say what she means. She protests that she means what she says—which, according to her, is the same thing. To this the Mad Hatter and the others reply:

> "Not the same thing a bit!" said the Hatter. "Why, you might just as well say that 'I see what I eat' is the same thing as 'I eat what I see'!"
> "You might just as well say," added the March Hare, "that 'I like what I get' is the same thing as 'I get what I like'!"
> "You might just as well say," added the Dormouse, which seemed to be talking in its sleep, "that 'I breathe when I sleep' is the same thing as 'I sleep when I breathe'!"

Unlike the E and I propositions, the A proposition does not have a valid converse. But we can validly convert the A if we limit its inference to an I proposition. From "All ball players exercise daily," it doesn't follow that "All those who exercise daily are ball players." But it does follow that "Some of those who exercise daily are ball players." This works because of the nature of the two types of propositions involved, the A and the I. The A proposition tells us that all of the members of the subject class, "ball players," are also members of another class, "those who exercise daily." It leaves open the possibility that there may be other members of that latter class who are not members of the first class. It asserts that *some* of the members of the latter class are members of the former class. If that is so, then we are justified in inferring from "All ball players exercise daily" that "Some of those who exercise daily are ball players." The A proposition, therefore, can always be validly converted by limitation to an I.

Let us now consider the O proposition. Given that "Some flowers are not roses," can we infer that "Some roses are not flowers"? Obviously we cannot.

The former proposition is true while the latter, its converse, is false. Similarly, given that "Some women are not mothers," can we infer that "Some mothers are not women"? Again, obviously not. The O proposition, in short, has no valid converse. The reason for this is that the O proposition asserts that some members of the subject class are excluded from the whole of the predicate class, or that some S's (these particular ones) do not belong to the whole of the P's. It is a proposition concerned with part of the S class and the whole of the P class. If this is so, we cannot turn this type of proposition around and assert that some P's do not belong to the *whole* of the S's. The original proposition provided us with no such information; it told us only about a portion of the S class, not the whole of it.

From the E proposition "No (S) is (P)," and the I proposition "Some (S) is (P)," we may validly infer, respectively, that "No (P) is (S)" and "Some (P) is (S)." From the A proposition "All (S) is (P)," we may validly infer that "Some (P) is (S)." And from the O proposition "Some (S) is not (P)," we cannot validly infer that "Some (P) is not (S)." It is possible to think of O propositions in which, if the original is true, its converse might also be true. For example, look at "Some voters are not in favor of busing." We would probably be justified in inferring that "Some people in favor of busing are not voters," but we would do so on the basis of our knowledge, not on the basis of logic. We simply happen to know that while some voters are not in favor of busing, some of those who are in favor of busing are not voters. In considering the relationships that hold logically between propositions, however, we are concerned with knowledge we can infer on the basis of logic alone, not on the basis of outside information we may have.

3. OBVERSION

Another logical relation between propositions is *obversion*." To *obvert* a proposition is to change its quality without changing its logical import. It is essentially changing an affirmative proposition to a negative one, or vice versa. In this process the subject term remains unchanged, but in order to preserve the original meaning we must change the predicate term to its opposite.

Let us see how this applies to the four categorical propositions, remembering that two separate operations are involved in obversion: (1) changing the quality of the proposition, and (2) changing the predicate term to its opposite. Basically an A obverts to an E, and an E to an A. An I obverts to an O, and an O to an I. Always maintain the quantity of the original proposition.

Following these steps we find that the obverse of the A proposition "All men are mortal" is "No men are immortal." The "All . . . is . . ." is changed to "No . . . is . . ." and the predicate term "mortal" is changed to its opposite, "immortal."

Obverting the E proposition "No essays are legible," we will get "All essays are illegible." Here again, the "No . . . is . . ." has become "All . . . is . . ." and the predicate term "legible" has become "illegible."

Obverting the I proposition "Some foods are tasty," we get its logical equivalent, "Some foods are not non-tasty." We could have phrased this "Some foods are not not tasty," but this would be awkward. It is better, whenever possible, to use the term *non-* rather than *not* when obverting, reserving the term *not* for use in the copula in O propositions.

It would also have been possible here to use a more colloquial expression, "tasteless," instead of the "non-" compound, as we did in our two previous examples ("illegible" and "immortal"). We must be cautious, however, since many apparent antonyms have acquired additional meanings and are no longer the strict negations they originally were. While this may not be so apparent with the terms "tasty" and "tasteless," consider the words "moral" and "immoral." The latter term doesn't merely assert the absence of a certain quality (as the term "non-moral" would) but rather has come to have separate and distinguishable characteristics of its own.

When negating the predicate term, be careful to place the negative sign in the proper place, especially if the negative term is a phrase consisting of several words. For example, if the proposition to be obverted is "All living beings are subject to pain and suffering," put the negative before the word "subject," so that the obverted proposition reads "No living being is one who is non-subject to pain and suffering," and not before the word "pain" (which would result in "No living being is one who is subject to non-pain and suffering").

Let us consider, finally, the O proposition. Obverting the proposition "Some books are not costly," we get "Some books are non-costly." The "Some . . . are not . . ." changes to "Some . . . are . . ." and the "costly" changes to "non-costly." Sometimes with terms like "costly," "poor," "good," it is tempting to replace them with their presumed opposites cheap, rich, or bad. But "cheap" is not the logical opposite, or *contradictory,* of "costly," and "rich" and "bad" are not the contradictories of "poor" and "good." These are merely the *contraries* of the original terms. (Two terms are *contradictory* if they are exhaustive as well as exclusive; two terms are *contrary* if they are simply exclusive. If something is costly it obviously cannot be cheap, so these two are exclusive. But since it is possible for the thing in question to be neither costly nor cheap, they are not exhaustive.)

4. CONTRAPOSITION

Combining conversion and obversion, we get additional types of inferences. Logicians have named these the *obverted converse* (which is an original proposition which has been converted and then obverted), the *partial contrapositive,* the *full contrapositive,* the *partial inverse,* and the *full inverse.* Of these combinations, the one that interests us most is the full contrapositive because we use it frequently with the A proposition. Since it is the only one we will consider, let us simply call it the *contrapositive*.

To derive the contrapositive, let us take as our example the proposition (1) "All Americans are literate." Obverting this proposition, we obtain (2) "No Americans are illiterate." Converting that, we get (3) "No illiterate persons are Americans." Obverting again, we obtain (4) "All illiterate persons are non-Americans." This last proposition (4)—which is the obverse of the converse of the obverse of the original—is the contrapositive of (1). Symbolically, the contrapositive of "All (S) is (P)" is, as we see, "All (non-P) is (non-S)."

This is a very useful equivalence, and is not hard to learn. Comparing the two as represented symbolically—All (S) is (P)↔All (non-P) is (non-S)—it becomes apparent that two things are required to obtain the contrapositive of the A proposition: (1) to interchange the S and P terms, and (2) to negate each of them. Seeing the derivation in this way also makes it clearer what it is we do when we err in deriving it. We have a tendency to go from "All (S) is (P)" to "All (non-S) is (non-P)," which is fallacious. From "All Americans are literate," we may indeed infer that "All those who are illiterate are non-Americans." But we may not infer from it that "All non-Americans are illiterate," for there are many other people besides Americans who are literate, and the original proposition did not intend to deny this.

Some people exploit the tendency to infer more than the words spoken actually imply or justify. "All contributors," we will be told, "show by their contribution that they care about their fellow human beings." Does this mean that "All non-contributors do not care about their fellow human beings"? Logically, of course, the first statement does not establish the second one at all, but this implication could be exploited to increase the number of contributors.

The philosopher John Locke appears to have made this mistake in a passage in his essay "Of Property," which, abridged, runs as follows:[1]

> The materials of nature (air, earth, water) that remain untouched by human effort belong to no one and are not property. It follows that a thing can become someone's private property only if he works and labors on it to change its natural state. From this I conclude that whatever a man improves by the labor of his hand and brain belongs to him, and to him only.

What Locke appears to be saying here is as follows:

1. If a thing is not worked on, it is not property
2. If it is property, then it is worked on
3. If it is worked on, then it is property

1. Quoted in Stephen N. Thomas, *Practical Reasoning in Natural Language*, 3rd ed. (Englewood Cliffs, N.J.: Prentice-Hall, 1986), pp. 206–7.

Although proposition 2 is a valid contrapositive of proposition 1, proposition 3 is not and does not logically follow from it. (Proposition 3 is the false converse of proposition 2.)

The contrapositive is possible only with the A and O propositions. It is valid for the E proposition only by limitation, and is not valid at all for I propositions. This is because contraposition involves the processes of obversion and conversion, and to achieve these in the case of the E and I propositions would involve converting either an A or an O proposition. The A can only be converted by limitation to an I, and the O cannot be converted at all.

5. DISTRIBUTION OF TERMS

Before considering other types of immediate inferences, we need to look at a technical matter concerning the four categorical propositions. Called *distribution of terms,* it is concerned with three points: the classes designated by the terms, whether or not those classes are occupied, and to what extent they are occupied.

A reference is made in the four categorical propositions regarding the classes designated by their terms. We want to know whether the reference is to the whole class or only to part of the class. If it is to the whole class, then the class is said to be *distributed;* if the reference is only to part of the class, the class is *undistributed.*

The A proposition asserts that every member of the subject class is a member of the predicate class. Since reference is made to every member of the subject class, the subject term is *distributed.* But is reference being made to every member of the predicate class? The answer is no. If I say, for example, "All artists are eccentric," I am not asserting that *only* artists are eccentric, nor am I saying that artists make up the *whole* class of eccentric people. I am only asserting that if a person is an artist, he is eccentric. But other people may be eccentric too, so the predicate term of the A proposition is *undistributed.*

We can now see more clearly why the A proposition does not convert simply, but rather only by limitation, to an I. The A proposition has a distributed subject and an undistributed predicate. In conversion, the predicate becomes the subject, and what was undistributed in the original is now distributed. Such an inference is invalid, since this would be equivalent to jumping from a knowledge of *some* things to a presumed knowledge of *all* things.

Like the A, the E proposition's quantifier makes reference (albeit in a negative way) to every member of the subject class. Unlike the A, however, the E states that not a single member of the S class is a member of the P class; thus the reference is to the whole of the predicate class. How could it maintain this to be so unless the *whole* of that class was surveyed and no S was found in it? Therefore, the predicate term in the E proposition is distributed. And because both terms are distributed, that proposition, unlike the A, converts simply.

In the I proposition, the quantifier makes it clear that only some members of the subject class are in discussion, so the subject is undistributed. But is the predicate term similarly undistributed? The answer is yes, since reference is being made here only to some members of that class, not to the whole of it. In a proposition like "Some men are wealthy," we need to identify only those members of the predicate class who are also members of the subject class; we are not concerned about the rest of the P class, which may be coextensive with other types of subject classes (for example, women who are wealthy).

Because both classes in the I proposition share the same kind of distribution, it can be converted simply. In interchanging the subject and predicate terms, as is required by the process of conversion, we are not going from an undistributed term (involving knowledge only about "some") to a distributed one (involving knowledge about "all"), as we would if we attempted to convert the A proposition simply.

As in the I, the quantifier "some" in the O proposition indicates that reference is being made to only a part of that class. The subject term of the O proposition is therefore undistributed. Is the predicate term also undistributed? The answer is no. The P term is distributed because if something is *excluded* from a class, the whole of the class is necessarily involved. How would we know that a certain S is not a member of a certain P class unless we had surveyed that whole P class and failed to find it there?

Because of its distribution, the O proposition cannot be validly converted. To convert it would involve transposing the S term to the P position, a position that is distributed, and the data of the original does not justify this. It would mean using the knowledge of only *some* to claim knowledge about *all*.

The following table illustrates the distribution situation for subject and predicate terms in each of the four categorical propositions:

Proposition Form	Subject Term	Predicate Term
A	D	U
E	D	D
I	U	U
O	U	D

Notice the symmetry between the A and O forms and between the E and I forms in this representation.

The subject of distribution can be difficult. The distribution of the subject term, however, is indicated clearly by the quantifier and should therefore offer no problems. As far as the predicate term is concerned, it may be helpful to remember that it is distributed only in the negative propositions (the E and O).

6. VENN DIAGRAMS

To see more clearly the importance of each of the four classical categorical propositions and the logical relationships between them, let us look at a device invented for this purpose in 1881 by the English mathematician and logician John

Venn (1834–1923). The device, called the *Venn diagram,* is similar to the Euler circles we looked at in Chapter One. The Venn diagrams use shading to indicate that a region is empty of members, and use numbers in the regions of the overlapping circles for easier identification. (If a region is not shaded and does not contain an X to indicate the presence of members, this indicates that nothing is known about the area; that is, it may or may not contain members.)

In the two overlapping circles shown here, for example,

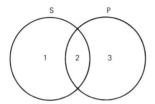

region 1 represents the area where we will find S's but not P's; region 2 represents the area where all the S's are P's and vice versa; and region 3 represents the area where there are P's but no S's. Placing an X in any of these areas would indicate the presence there of members; shading any of these areas would indicate the absence of members.

Let us now look at the four categorical propositions in their Venn diagram form.

The A proposition "All (S) is (P)" asserts that all of the S's are P's. To represent this in Venn diagram form, we need to shade out region 1:

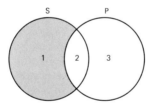

That region is shaded because, if all S's are P's, then there are no S's outside the P's. The shaded region contains the S's that are not P's.

The E proposition "No (S) is (P)" asserts that there are no S's that are P's, and to represent that with a Venn diagram we shade out the area that contains S's that *are* P's:

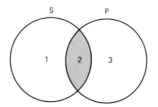

This is an accurate pictorial representation of the E proposition.

Another important point is that neither the A nor the E proposition asserts that its members exist. But since such members (with rare exceptions) *will* exist, we indicate this by placing a circled X in region 2 of the A proposition:

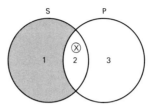

and a circled X in region 3 of the E proposition.

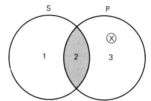

We will discuss this further later in the chapter:

The I proposition ''Some (S) is (P)'' asserts that there are S's that are P's. In a Venn diagram, we would simply place an X in region 2 where we find both S's and P's:

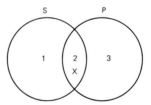

Region 1 is not shaded and does not contain an X to indicate the presence of members, because with this proposition we don't know what the situation in that region is—it may or may not contain members.

Finally, the O proposition ''Some (S) is not (P)'' asserts that there are some S's outside the area of the P's. Therefore, in the Venn diagram, we place an X in region 1:

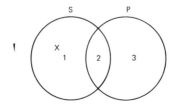

Region 2 is left blank, since the proposition tells us nothing about it.

Let's see what happens when we apply this technique to the relations of propositions. If the operations of conversion, obversion, and contraposition result in true equivalences—if, for example "Some (S) is (P)" is truly equivalent to "Some (P) is (S)"—it should be apparent pictorially. Let us see whether this is so.

When expressed in Venn diagram form, proposition I ("Some (S) is (P)") consisted of two interesting circles with an X in region 2, identifying the S's that are also P's:

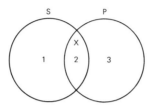

The converse of this proposition—"Some (P) is (S)"—is in effect the same illustration.

In the Venn diagram of the E proposition, region 2 was shaded out to tell us that there were no S's that were P's:

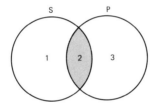

Here too, if we diagrammed the converse of that proposition—"No (P) is (S)"—we would draw the same illustration. These diagrams confirm that we can validly convert both the I and E propositions "simply."

The case, however, is different with the diagram of the A proposition "All (S) is (P)," which has region 1 shaded out:

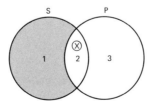

Visually, its converse—"All (P) is (S)"—would show shading in region 3, not region 1.

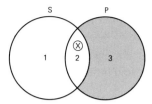

The difference between these two diagrams illustrates that the two propositions are not equivalent.

We can, however, convert the A proposition (by limitation) to an I: ''Some (P) is (S).'' This inference is valid but not strictly equivalent, as the diagram shows.

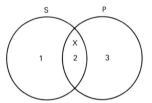

This diagram isn't identical with the original, but neither is it incompatible. The original had region 1 shaded out to indicate the absence of members there, and a circled X in region 2 to indicate that if there were S's, that is where they would be. The new proposition—''Some (P) is (S)''—now informs us that such S's exist, and this is shown in the Venn diagram.

In the O proposition ''Some (S) is not (P),'' the original is represented pictorially as follows:

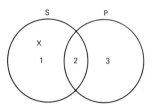

That is quite different from the diagram of its converse—''Some (P) is not (S):

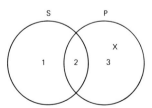

This confirms that the O proposition cannot be converted.

Applying the Venn diagram method to the logical relationship of obversion, we see that these are equivalent propositions, and that the logical operation used to arrive at them is valid.

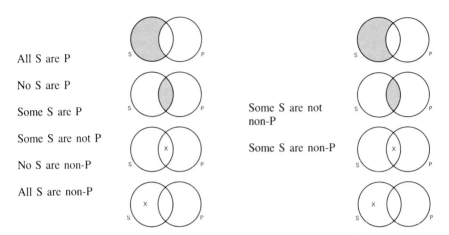

All S are P

No S are P

Some S are P

Some S are not P

No S are non-P

All S are non-P

Some S are not non-P

Some S are non-P

The same is true of the contrapositive of the A proposition, as the Venn diagrams show:

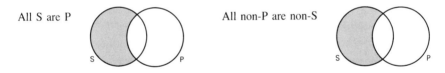

All S are P

All non-P are non-S

7. SQUARE OF OPPOSITION

In relating the four categorical propositions to each other, no operations will be performed on them, but we will consider the following question: Given that one of these four propositions is true or false, what is the case with the remaining three?

For example, if the A proposition "All men are wise" is true, how does it affect the truth or falsity of the propositions "No men are wise," "Some men are wise," and "Some men are not wise"? Are they also true or are they all false? And if some are true and some false, which are which, and why?

To see these relationships more clearly, we can use the ingenious device invented by Aristotle called the *square of opposition*. The square is helpful both as an illustration of the various relations and as a source of reference.

As shown in the illustration, the corners of the square represent each of the four categorical propositions. The two universals occupy the top corners and the two particulars the bottom ones. They are arranged so that the two affirmative propositions are on the left side of the square and the two negative ones are on the right side:

Let us begin with the most basic of relations, that of contradiction. If someone maintained that "All men are wise" was true and we wished to challenge him, what would we say in opposition? Would we refute it with the E or the O proposition? Of course we wouldn't use the I ("Some men are wise"), because it would be a weak argument.

The tendency is to oppose the A with the E. If someone claims that "All men are wise," we are inclined to respond in kind by replying that "No men are wise." A moment's thought, however, will show that this is not the strongest response available to us, and that in fact, though opposed to what the first speaker offered, the response does not necessarily confirm what is offered by us. Is it not possible that it is neither true that "All men are wise" nor that "No men are wise," for the fact is simply that some are wise and some are not. If this is so, then both of us may be mistaken. In opposing the A with an E, we overstated our case. To refute the contention that all men are wise, all we needed to do was to find just one person who was not wise. The true contradictory of "all," then, is "some," not "none." The contradictory of the A proposition, therefore, is the O, not the E. (And similarly, the contradictory of the E proposition is the I.) As the following diagram illustrates, the contradictories occupy the extreme corners of the square:

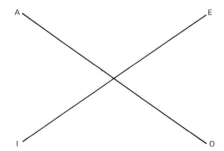

Contradiction is the clearest and strictest kind of relation. The truth of one proposition necessitates the falsity of the other, and vice versa. It describes a situation between two propositions in which both cannot be true and both cannot be false; that if one is true, the other must be false, and if one is false, the other must be true.

The Venn diagram clearly illustrates this relation. In the A proposition, region 1 is empty, but the region is occupied in A's contradictory, the O proposition. In the E proposition, region 2 is now empty but is occupied in E's contradictory, the I proposition:

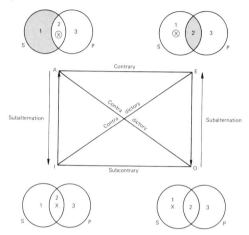

The alternatives described by contradiction, to explain it in another way, are both exclusive and exhaustive. They cover all the cases there are and assert that it must be one or the other. This is not the situation with the relation between the A and the E propositions. Although both of them cannot be true together, both may very well be false. These two propositions are called *contraries.*

The opposition between contraries is not as complete as that existing between contradictories. In a controversy, if we are able to produce evidence that contradicts our opponent's position, then we have established our own position. If, however, we oppose that position only with a contrary one, we may mistakenly think we have refuted our opponent when we haven't, since both positions may be false (the truth lying somewhere in between). Two propositions are logical contraries, then, when both cannot be true but both may be false. Given either as true, we may infer that the other is false; but given one as false, the truth-value of the other is still undetermined. That is, we have no way of knowing whether it is true or false except through additional information.

Arguments often prove fruitless (as well as endless) because of a tendency to confuse contraries with contradictories. One party maintains that all men are basically egoists, the other claims that none really are. One party maintains heredity is everything, the other insists that environment is. Each sees the falsity of the other's position, but not of his own. When two propositions contradict, one of them must be true; but when two propositions are merely contrary, they cannot both be true, though both may be false.

Venn diagrams clearly illustrate this. We can see from the representation of A and E that both cannot be true. One says that an area (region 1) is empty, while the other says that it is not. On the other hand, both may be false, since it may be the case (as the diagram shows) that some men are wise (Some S is P) and some men are not wise (Some S is not P).

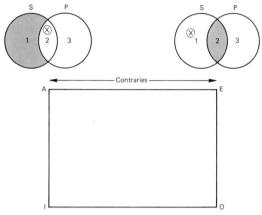

In contrast to the relationship between the A and the E is that known as *subcontrariety*, which defines the relationship of I and O. With contrariety both propositions may be false, although both cannot be true. With subcontrariety both may be true, but both cannot be false. The I and O propositions are such subcontraries. If it is false that "Some men are wise" (I), then it must be true that "Some men are not wise" (O); and if it is false that "Some men are not wise" (O), then it must be true that "Some men are wise" (I). But if it is true that "Some men are wise" (I), then we do not really know whether "Some men are not wise" (O) is true or false. The original statement, "Some men are wise," could mean as few as one or as many as all.

This can be shown by Venn diagrams depicting these two propositions and their relations to each other:

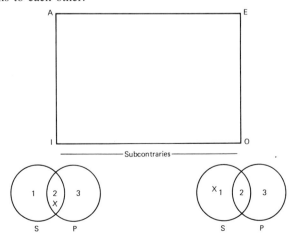

Both may be true since the I states that region 2 is occupied, and the O states that region 1 is occupied—a compatible situation. On the other hand, if the I were false, region 2 would be shaded to indicate that it is empty. The remaining S's would have to be located in region 1.

The popular expression "Life is full of contradictions" would probably be more accurate if the term "subcontraries" replaced the term "contradictions." The maxim tries to express the thought that in life many different things can coexist. While this is true of subcontraries (both may be true although both cannot be false), it is not true of contradictories (where both can neither be true nor false together).

Another relation between propositions is that of *implication*. This is the relationship in which the A (or E) stands to the I (or O), and the I (or O) to the A (or E). The relationship between the A and the I (or the E and the O) is called *superimplication*. The A is the *superimplicant* and the I its *superimplicate*. The relationship between the I and the A (or the O and the E) is called *subimplication*. The I is the *subimplicant* and the A its *subimplicate*. (Frequently the relation of implication is called *subalternation*. In this case A is the *superalternate* of I, and E is the superalternate of O, while I is the *subalternate* of A, and O the subalternate of E.)

Superimplication is easy to determine. If it is true that "All men are wise," then it must be true that *some* are. The same applies to E: If it is true that "No men are wise," then it must be equally true that some are not. If the A is true, then the I is true; and if the E is true, then the O is true. On the other hand, if it is false that "All men are wise," is it also false that "Some men are wise"? Clearly not. It may be false that all men are wise but not false that *some* are. Therefore, is it *true* that some are? Here again the answer is no. We are simply not in a position to know. Thus, if the A is false the I is *undetermined*. The same applies to the E and O.

Subimplication is the relationship in which the I (or O) stands to the A (or E). If we know that "Some men are wise" is false, what do we know about its subimplicate, the A? Can we know that it is equally false? The answer is yes, because if it is false that "Some men are wise," how can it be true that all of them are? The same applies to the relationship between the O and the E.

But suppose it is true that "Some men are wise." Must it also be true that all of them are? It could be that they are, but perhaps they are not; given that some are wise, we simply do not know whether the rest are or are not. Therefore, it is undetermined. (The same applies to the relationship between the O and E, given that the O is true.) Venn diagrams clearly illustrate these points. (See diagram on p. 32.)

If the A proposition is true, then region 2 has at least one member, and this is what is asserted by the I proposition, as the diagram for that proposition indeed shows. By similar reasoning, if the E proposition is true, then the O proposition is also true. Conversely, if the I proposition is false, then region 2 of the S circle is empty, making the A assertion false. And if the O proposition is false, then

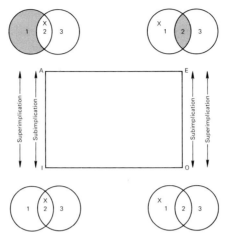

region 1 of the S circle is empty, making the E proposition false (as the diagrams show would indeed be the case).

Superimplication and subimplication tell us the following about their respective propositions:

> If A is true, I is true.
> If E is true, O is true.
> If A is false, I is undetermined.
> If E is false, O is undetermined.

Further,

> If I is false, A is false.
> If O is false, E is false.
> If I is true, A is undetermined.
> If O is true, E is undetermined.

Combining these with earlier results we discovered with contradiction, contrary, and subcontrary relationships , we obtain the following table of values:

> If A is given as true, then: E is false, I is true, O is false.
> If E is given as true, then: A is false, I is false, O is true.
> If I is given as true, then: E is false, A is undetermined, O is undetermined.
> If O is given as true, then: A is false, E is undetermined, I is undetermined.
> If A is given as false, then: E is undetermined, I is undetermined, O is true.
> If E is given as false, then: A is undetermined, I is true, O is undetermined.
> If I is given as false, then: A is false, E is true, O is true.
> If O is given as false, then: A is true, E is false, I is true.

The purpose of the square of opposition was to make this data more accessible, almost automatic. This data can be even more accessible if one takes a few shortcuts. One shortcut involves the relationships of contradiction and implication. For example, if we know that the A is true, then we know that the O, its contradictory, is false; and if the A is true, then its superimplicate, the I, must also be true. And if the I is true, then the E, *its* contradictory, must be false. So, from knowing the A is true, we automatically know about the other three propositions. The same is true of the other universal proposition, the E.

With the particular propositions, if we know that the I is false, then we know that the E, its contradictory, is true. If we know the E is true, then we know that the O (its superimplicate) must be true; and if *it* is true, then we know *its* contradictory, the A, must be false. So from knowing that the I is false (and knowing only the relationships of contradiction and superimplication), we know whether the other three propositions are true or false. The same is true of the other particular proposition, the O.

So far we have "worked" the square by assuming either that the A (or E) is true or that the I (or O) is false. What happens if we find ourselves in a reverse position? What if we know the falsity of a universal or the truth of a particular rather than the truth of a universal and the falsity of a particular?

Suppose that the A is false. In knowing only that, what can we know about the other three propositions? Let us work the square again. If the A is false, then we know that the O, its contradictory, must be true, but we do not really know whether its superimplicate, the I, is true or false. It may be true or false. All we can say is that it is undetermined; and if *it* is undetermined, then its contradictory, the E, must also be undetermined. So by knowing that the A is false, we know about the other three propositions. The same applies to its companion universal proposition, the E.

Suppose we know that the I is true. What about the remaining three propositions? If the I is true, then the E, its contradictory, must be false. If the E is false, its superimplicate, the O, must be undetermined. And if the O is undetermined, then the A, *its* contradictory, must also be undetermined. With a little practice you will be able to go through this square rapidly and easily.

8. EXISTENTIAL IMPORT

Finally, we have to consider a matter we touched on earlier. In the literature of logic, it is called the question of *existential import*. It is concerned with whether the A proposition "All (S) is (P)" is to be understood as entailing the existence of the members of the S class.

The I and O propositions assert, respectively, that "Some (S's) are (P's)" and "Some (S's) are not (P's)." The word "some" in these two propositions assumes that at least one of the things designated by the subject term actually exists. By implying that the classes designated by their subject terms are not empty, these propositions can be said to have existential import.

Traditional logic assumes or presupposes the existence of members in the subject classes of all four propositions and not just in the two particular ones. There would seem to be an important difference, however, between particular and universal categorical propositions on this question of existential import, since universal propositions leave open the possibility that the members of which they speak may not exist. For example, such propositions as "All bodies free of impressed forces will persevere in their states of rest or motion in a straight line forever" (Newton's First Law of Motion) and "All trespassers will be prosecuted" do not imply that there are such bodies or that there presently exist such violators. In the first case, there are no such bodies; in the second, the purpose of the assertion is to prevent its readers from becoming trespassers. In short, the "all" of the universal affirmative proposition (and the universal negative propositions) means "all that there are," and in fact there may be none.

These differences between the particular and universal propositions have led many modern logicians to interpret the universal propositions in a *hypothetical* rather than an *existential* way.

To understand the universal propositions in this way means that many inferences that we considered valid on our square of opposition will need to be revised, for these inferences are based on the traditional assumption that both universal and particular propositions imply class membership. If we assume now that the universals do not assume class membership, this would entail the following changes:

1. The relationship of superimplication would have to be denied. Given that "All (S) is (P)," we may not infer that "Some (S) is (P)," for "Some (S) is (P)" implies the existence of the S or S's, while "All (S) is (P)" does not.

2. The relationship of subimplication would have to be denied. Given that "Some (S) is (P)" is false, we may not infer that "All (S) is (P)" is false, since "All (S) is (P)" makes no assertion of existence asserted by the particular. The falsity of the particular, therefore, would not imply the falsity of the universal proposition.

3. The relationship of contrariety would have to be denied. If there are no S's, then there is nothing inconsistent in asserting both propositions. "All," as we saw, may mean "All that there are," or "none," and that is what the E asserts.

4. The relationship of subcontrariety would have to be denied. This would follow from the preceding, for if S does not exist, then both "Some (S) is (P)" and "Some (S) is not (P)" are false. (They cannot, therefore, be subcontraries, since subcontrariety is a relationship in which both cannot be false, although both may be true).

On the new interpretation, the I and O can no longer be derived from A and E, and vice versa. The A and E are not necessarily contraries, nor are the I and O necessarily subcontraries, since both of the former pair might be true and both of the latter false. In short, the only relationship that remains is that of contradiction.

These are the somewhat startling results that follow if we assume that universal propositions do not imply class membership, while particular propositions do. But we shouldn't entirely abandon this part of classical logic. The relations and inferences described by the square of opposition (and such a logical operation as the conversion by limitation of the A proposition) are still valid and useful. We must remember, however, that traditional logic assumes existential import, and therefore what it teaches us regarding these logical relations does not apply in the case of universal propositions whose classes are empty or null. Such examples will be rare, and some will turn on odd usage. An officer might report that "All trespassers were apprehended" and upon being asked how many there were, might reply "None." More likely, however, if there had been none to apprehend he would simply have said so.

SUMMARY

The ability to recognize the equivalence of statements and their relations to one another is very helpful in cutting through the verbiage surrounding arguments.

Propositions that have different subject and predicate terms are considered *independent*. The truth or falsity of one such proposition is unrelated to the truth or falsity of the other. *Dependent* propositions—those that share the same subject and predicate terms—stand in definite relationships to one another, and the truth or falsity of one can be inferred directly or immediately from the truth or falsity of another.

Among the two most basic of such relations are conversion and obversion. To *convert* a proposition means to interchange the position of the S and P terms. We thereby obtain a new proposition by immediate inference from the given one. The E and the I forms may both be converted "simply." For example, if we are given that "No cats are dogs," we may infer by conversion that "No dogs are cats."

The A form, however, cannot be converted simply. From "All ball players exercise daily," we cannot infer that "All who exercise daily are ball players." The A proposition can be validly converted by limitation to an I proposition. From "All ball players exercise daily," we can validly infer that "Some of those who exercise daily are ball players."

The O form cannot be converted at all. Given that "Some voters are not in favor of busing," we cannot tell (without additional information) whether "Some of those in favor of busing are not voters" is true or false.

To *obvert* a proposition is to change its "quality" without changing its logical import. An affirmative proposition obverts to a negative, and vice versa. In this process the subject term remains unchanged, but (in order to preserve the original meaning) we must change the predicate term to its opposite or contradictory. For example, "All essays are illegible" obverts to "No essays are legible." If we symbolize the original predicate by "P," we may symbolize the opposite or contradictory by "non-P." Therefore, the obverse of "All (S) is (P)" is "No (S) is (non-P)"; the obverse of "No (S) is (P)" is "All (S) is (non-P)"; that of "Some (S) is (P)" is "Some (S) is not (non-P)"; and that of "Some (S) is not (P)" is "Some (S) is (non-P)."

By combining the two operations of conversion and obversion, we get additional types of inferences. Of these, the most widely used and most interesting is the *contrapositive*. Symbolically, the contrapositive of "All (S) is (P)" is "All (non-P) is (non-S)." Although many people are tempted to infer "All (non-S) is (non-P)" from "All (S) is (P)," that inference is false.

Distribution of terms is an important feature of categorical propositions. A term is said to be *distributed* if we have information about every member of the class. If we have information only about some of the class, the term is *undistributed*. So the A proposition distributes its subject but not its predicate terms; the E distributes both its subject and predicate; the I distributes neither its subject nor its predicate; and the O distributes its predicate but not its subject. In short, the subject terms are distributed in the universal propositions (A and E) and only there; the predicate terms are distributed in the negative propositions (E and O) and only there.

The English mathematician John Venn invented a method for illustrating propositions and their various relationships. In Venn diagrams, numbers identify the separate regions of the overlapping circles, shading indicates that a region is empty of members, and X's denote the presence of members. Venn diagrams provide us with a striking and graphic test of validity of inference.

Five additional logical relations emerge when we consider the ways in which the four categorical propositions stand to one another when "S" and "P" denote the same classes throughout all four forms. These relationships are *contradiction, contrariety, subcontrariety, superimplication,* and *subimplication*.

Two propositions are logical *contradictories* when both cannot be true together and both cannot be false together. If one is true, the other must be false; if one is false, the other must be true. If it is true that "All men are wise," then it must be false that "Some men are not wise," and vice versa. A and O are thus contradictories, as are E and I.

Two propositions are logical *contraries* when both cannot be true but both may be false, as is the case with the A and E forms. Given either as true, we may infer that the other is false; but given one as false, the truth-value of the other is undetermined—we have no way of knowing whether it is true or false except through additional information.

Two propositions are logical *subcontraries* when both may be true but both cannot be false. This relation exists between the I and the O forms. If the I is false, the O is true; if the O is false, the I is true. But if one is true, the other is undetermined; without additional information we can't know whether it is true or false.

One proposition is said to be in the relation of *superimplication* to a second if the truth of the first implies the truth of the second. This is the relationship in which the A stands to the I and the E to the O. Given that the A is true, the I must be true. However, given that the A is false, the I is undetermined in the absence of additional information. The same applies to the relationship between the E and O.

Finally, the I stands to the A in the relationship of *subimplication*. Given that I is false, A must be false. Given, however, that the I is true, the A remains undetermined. The same applies to the E and O forms.

The square of opposition clarifies these relationships and makes derivation immediately possible. The two upper corners of the square represent the universal propositions (A and E) and the bottom two the particular propositions (I and O). The affirmative propositions (A and I) are on the left side of the square and the negative propositions (E and O) on the right side. The two upper corners represent the relation of contrariety, the lower that of subcontrariety. The left and right corners represent the relationships of superimplication and subimplication, respectively. The diagonally opposed corners represent the relationship of contradiction.

It is clear that the two particular propositions (I and O) imply that these members exist. Although there is some doubt as to whether all universal propositions imply class membership (that is, have such existential import), traditional logic assumes they do.

Exercises

I. Put each of the following propositions into proper class-analysis form and indicate its distribution. Where possible, give the converse and obverse of each. In the case of A propositions, state their contrapositive as well.

1. Some drugs are habit-forming.
2. No theory is irrefutable.
3. All tears are wet.
4. Few campaign promises are ever kept.
5. Some languages are hard to learn.
6. All life is sacred.
7. Some wounds never heal.
8. Not all people are ambitious.
9. Philosophy does not bake bread.
10. Power corrupts.

II. State the proposition represented in each of the following Venn diagrams.

11.

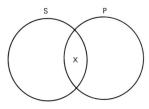

12.

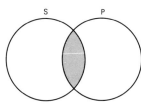

13.

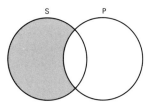

14.

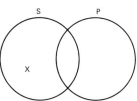

III. State the process (conversion, obversion, and so on) by which we pass from the original proposition "All S is P" to each of the following. (See answers in appendix.)

15. No S is non-P

16. Some P is S

17. Some S is not P

18. No S is P

19. Some S is P

20. All non-P is non-S

Do the same with the proposition "No S is P":

21. All S is P

22. All S is non-P

23. Some S is not P

24. No P is S

25. Some S is P

Do the same with the proposition "Some S is P":

26. All S is P

27. Some P is S

28. Some S is not non-P

29. Some S is not P

30. No S is P

And with the proposition "Some S is not P":

31. Some S is non-P

32. Some S is P

33. All S is P

34. No S is P

IV. Complete the following chart, using T, F, and U to symbolize *True, False,* and *Undetermined.* For example, if A is true, then its contradictory O must be false, its superimplicate I must be true, and its contrary E must be false.

35. If A is true, then I is _____, E is _____, O is _____
    If A is false, then I is _____, E is _____, O is _____

    If E is true, then A is _____, I is _____, O is _____
    If E is false, then A is _____, I is _____, O is _____

    If I is true, then A is _____, E is _____, O is _____
    If I is false, then A is _____, E is _____, O is _____

    If O is true, then A is _____, E is _____, I is _____
    If O is false, then A is _____, E is _____, O is _____

V. In the following exercise, translate each proposition into proper class-analysis form and then determine the relationship between each set of propositions. (See answers in appendix.)

36. No one who is not willing to die for his country can call himself a patriot.

    No one can call himself a patriot who is not willing to die for his country.

37. All who entered the race were from out of state.
    None who entered the race were from out of state.

38. Some players won't make it.
    Some will.

39. All the tickets are gone.
    None of the tickets are left.

40. All the young people voted for him.
    Among those who voted for him were many young people.

41. Only the brave deserve the fair.
    Some who deserve the fair are not brave.

42. Few streets are safe these days.
    No streets are safe these days.

43. No one is perfect.
    Some are not perfect.

44. Many of those on welfare are not unemployed.
    Some of those on welfare are employed.

45. None but seniors have been invited.
    If you're not a senior, you're not invited.

THREE

Syllogistic Reasoning

1. MEDIATE INFERENCE

As we learned in the last chapter, propositions that share the same subject and predicate terms are called dependent propositions. Although such propositions may differ in quantity (one may be universal, the other particular) and in quality (one may be negative, the other affirmative), the truth or falsity of one can be inferred directly or immediately from the truth or falsity of the other. For example, if it is true that "All men are mortal," we may infer that it is also true that some men are mortal and false that some men are not mortal.

There are more complex types of inference that cannot be drawn directly from the given premise but require the mediation of another premise. These are called *mediate inferences* in contrast to the "immediate" types we examined in the last chapter. The most common of these mediate inferences involve arguments consisting of two premises and a conclusion—the following, for example:

> All men are mortal
> Socrates is a man
> ———————————
> Socrates is mortal

The first person to study and systematize these types of inference was Aristotle. He called them *syllogisms,* from the Greek words *syn,* meaning "together," and *logizesthai,* meaning "to reason." Aristotle himself defined these forms of inference or reasoning as "discourse in which, certain things being posited, something else than what is posited necessarily follows merely from them.''

Aristotle's goal in studying these inferences was to discover precisely what is it that allows us to move from two such propositions (premises) to the third (conclusion). He realized that what justifies us is the existence of a strict identity between the items brought together. From the premise ''All men are mortal,'' we may confidently conclude that ''Socrates is mortal'' because that first premise implies a second premise. That is, Socrates is a man, and hence like all other men must be mortal. A conclusion such as this is easily accepted, since it is already present in the original premise. And it is indeed only when nothing appears in the conclusion that did not first appear in the premises that we can confidently assert that conclusion. Under other circumstances we can never be certain our inferences are valid.

This shows us how strict the conditions of validity are, and what internal connections govern it. It also shows us how little we accomplish when we prove something—that is, show something to be ''valid.''

Aristotle came to see all this as a result of his observation of the structure of the syllogism. The seventeenth-century German philosopher Gottfried Leibniz described this discovery as ''one of the most beautiful, and one of the most important, made by the human mind.''

2. SYLLOGISMS

We observed earlier that thinking is a matter of combining words in propositions. Although, given the number of words at our disposal, we can generate an almost endless number of propositions, the number of types we can generate is severely limited. Of these types, logicians have isolated three in particular: the *categorical,* the *hypothetical,* and the *disjunctive propositions.*

These three main types of propositions give rise to three main types of syllogisms—the categorical, the hypothetical, and the disjunctive syllogisms. The categorical, which is composed entirely of categorical propositions, is sometimes also called the *Aristotelian syllogism,* because it was the only type recognized by Aristotle. The larger part of the classical doctrine of the syllogism is devoted to the categorical type, and we shall confine our attention here entirely to it.

3. THE STRUCTURE OF THE CATEGORICAL SYLLOGISM

A categorical syllogism may be defined as a form of argument consisting of three categorical propositions which contain between them three and only three terms. Two of the propositions are premises and the third is the conclusion. The inference attempts to discover the relations in which two of the terms stand to each other by observing the relations in which each stands to a third, or mediate, term.

These parts of the syllogism are called, respectively, the *major,* the *minor,* and the *middle terms.* The two premises from which the conclusion is inferred are called the *major* and *minor premises.* See the following syllogism:

> All (things that are excellent) are (things that are rare)
> All (wisdom) is (a thing that is excellent)
> _____
> All (wisdom) is (a thing that is rare)

The *major term* is the term that appears as the predicate of the conclusion—namely, "a thing that is rare." The *minor term* is the term that appears as the subject of the conclusion—namely, "wisdom." The *middle term* is the remaining term which does not appear in the conclusion but occurs in each premise—namely, "things that are excellent." Further, the *major premise* is the premise that contains the major term—in this syllogism, "All (things that are excellent) are (things that are rare)." The *minor premise* contains the minor term—here, "All (wisdom) is (a thing that is excellent)." The *conclusion,* of course, is the remaining proposition—"All (wisdom) is (a thing that is rare)."

Logicians symbolize the major term by the letter P (for *predicate*), the minor term by the letter S (*subject*), and the middle term by the letter M. They always write the major premise first, although in everyday discourse we tend to state our premises (as well as our conclusions) in any order we choose.

Attaching the symbols S, P, and M to the terms of our syllogism, it looks like this:

> **M**   **P**
> All (things that are excellent) are (things that are rare)
>   **S**   **M**
> All (wisdom) is (a thing that is excellent)
> _____
>   **S**   **P**
> All (wisdom) is (a thing that is rare)

Extracting the symbols from the syllogism, we see the following logical structure:

> All M are P
> All S are M
> _____
> All S are P

It is this logical structure that interests the logician, because a syllogism's validity doesn't depend on *what* it talks about (what S, P, and M stand for) but rather on the *way* it does so (how S, P, and M are combined). In short, it depends on the structure. But the example above is only one of many possible structures. Classical logic tries to determine the other structures and their validity.

Let us summarize what we have learned so far. A categorical syllogism consists of two premises related in a way that entails a certain conclusion. These two premises have a total of three terms. From the relation of two of them to the third, the relation of these two to each other can be determined. These two terms are the subject term and the predicate term, and the third is the middle term. Although the middle term does not appear in the conclusion, the conclusion can be reached only through its mediation. This type of inference is called *mediate inference,* to distinguish it from immediate inference, in which no mediating or middle term is required.

4. FIGURE AND MOOD OF THE CATEGORICAL SYLLOGISM

Although on first thought it might appear that one could construct innumerable syllogisms, the actual number is relatively small and can be precisely determined.

This can be done in the following fashion. In the previous example, the major premise was an A proposition (namely, ''All M is P''); however, it might have been an E (''No M is P''), an I (''Some M is P''), or an O (''Some M is not P''). The same is true of the minor premise ''All S is M''; it too could have been an E (''No S is M''), an I (''Some S is M''), or an O (''Some S is not M''). Since each of these four major premises could be combined with any one of the four minor premises, the number of combinations of syllogisms is now sixteen (4×4).

What we have said about each premise applies to the conclusion as well. In our example it happens to be an A proposition (''All S is P''), but it could also have been an E (''No S is P''), an I (''Some S is P''), or an O (''Some S is not P''). By combining these four possible conclusions with the sixteen possible combinations of premises, we arrive at a total of sixty-four ($4 \times 4 \times 4$) possible types of syllogisms.

These various combinations of A, E, I, and O propositions are known as the *mood* of the syllogism. This mood is determined by the type and combination of the categorical propositions that make up the syllogism. The mood of a syllogism is traditionally represented by three letters. The first names the form of the syllogism's major premise, the second that of the minor premise, and the third that of the conclusion. The mood of our example would therefore be represented as AAA.

Given that we can have four kinds of premises and conclusions, there are at least sixty-four different types of syllogisms possible ($4 \times 4 \times 4$). These do not represent all of the possibilities. One additional factor is the position of the middle term in the syllogism. In our example, the middle term fell on the subject side of the major premise (''All M is P'') and on the predicate side of the minor premise (''All S is M''), giving rise to the following pattern:

All M is P
All S is M

But both could have fallen on the predicate side of each of the premises, giving rise to this pattern:

All P is M
All S is M

Similarly, both could have fallen on the subject side of each of the premises, as follows:

All M is P
All M is S

Finally, the middle term could have fallen on the predicate side of the major premise and on the subject side of the minor, thus:

All P is M
All M is S

The result is four different *figures,* as these are called.

By combining these four possibilities with each of the sixty-four already determined, we arrive at a total number of 256 syllogisms. And, as Aristotle discovered, this is the exact number of forms the syllogism can take—that is, the total number of ways we can argue syllogistically.

To distinguish between them and to recall them more easily, generations of students have drawn lines connecting the different positions of the middle term in each of the four figures, to form something resembling the letter W or the collar of a shirt:

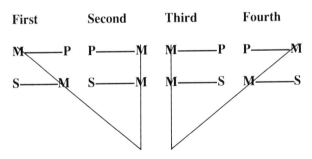

Together with its mood and figure, the form of a categorical syllogism can be completely specified. This is done by listing its mood (for example, AAA) and figure (AAA-1). Such a classification is analogous to the two principles of quantity and quality used to analyze propositions. One of these alone is insufficient to specify the type of syllogism in question.

Of the 256 types of syllogisms, which are valid and why? Actually, it may surprise you that only 24 are valid—and on a stricter interpretation, only 15.

Ordinarily we do not express ourselves syllogistically, so before we can learn how to determine validity, we need to learn how to transcribe our usual means of expression into proper syllogistic form.

5. TRANSLATING ORDINARY ARGUMENTS INTO SYLLOGISTIC FORM

Arguments, as ordinarily expressed, are often unorganized, verbose, and repetitive. Conclusions are not clearly distinguishable from premises, one or the other is frequently omitted or highly abbreviated, and both are usually encumbered with distracting and irrelevant considerations. Such arguments cannot be ascribed to one of the 256 types until they are expressed in proper syllogistic form. Propositions, as we saw earlier, are burdened with similar difficulties. We have to scrape away irrelevancies, reduce verbiage, and pull various strands together until we are left with three constituent propositions—two representing the argument's premises and the third its conclusion, all expressed in proper class-analysis form.

This is by far the most difficult part of the analysis, but there are steps to make it easier. The first and perhaps most important step is to find the conclusion of the proposed argument. It will not always be stated after the premises. Frequently a person will state the conclusion first and then go on to state the reasons or premises; or he or she will state one premise, then the conclusion, and then the other premise. To determine the conclusion of the argument, look for such expressions as "therefore," "hence," "so," and "consequently." Premises will be introduced by terms such as "because," "for," "since," and "on the ground that." When an argument lacks these indicators, you may find its conclusion by a process of elimination, or by trying to determine what the main thrust and direction of the argument is.

Having determined the argument's conclusion, your next step is to rewrite the argument, putting the conclusion last. This is especially helpful with a complicated and lengthy argument which requires heavy editing before it can be expressed in proper class-analysis form. Where the argument is not especially verbose or complicated, it might be sufficient simply to underline the conclusion within the text and proceed to the next step.

With the argument now reduced to manageable form, the next step is to put it in the form of a syllogism, with the major premise first, followed by the minor premise, and finally the conclusion. The terms must then be symbolized, by placing the letters S, P, and M above the appropriate terms.

The last step (before evaluating the argument against the rules of validity) is to symbolize its form by abstracting the S, P, and M terms and adding to them their respective distribution.

Let us take the steps just outlined, using the following abbreviated argument as our first example:

> All of these people must be communists, for all of them are socialists and all communists are socialists.

First, find the conclusion of the argument. The example above does not contain indicators like "therefore," "hence," or "consequently." It does contain, however, the term "for," which tells us that the proposition "all of them are socialists" is intended to be a premise. The word "and" ties that proposition to the next one, "all communists are socialists," and therefore seems to be a premise as well. If that is so, then the remaining proposition, "all of these people must be communists," must be, by process of elimination, the conclusion of the argument. This is even more likely since the main thrust of the argument is indicated by the word "must."

Now that we have determined what the conclusion of the argument is, our next step is to express it in proper syllogistic form, remembering to put the major premise first and conclusion last. This gives us the following result:

> All (communists) are (socialists)
> All (of these people) are (socialists)
> _____
> All (of these people) are (communists)

The third step is to symbolize the terms of the argument, placing the letters S, P, and M above their respective terms, as follows:

$$\text{All (communists)}^{P} \text{ are (socialists)}^{M}$$
$$\text{All (of these people)}^{S} \text{ are (socialists)}^{M}$$
$$\overline{\text{All (of these people)}^{S} \text{ are (communists)}^{P}}$$

Having done so, we must next symbolize the form of the argument by extracting its structure from it, thus:

> All P are M
> All S are M
> _____
> All S are P

The next step is to write in the distribution. Since both premises and conclusion are A propositions, the distribution will be the same in all three propositions:

$$
\begin{array}{cc}
\mathbf{D} & \mathbf{U} \\
\text{All P} & \text{are M} \\
\mathbf{D} & \mathbf{U} \\
\text{All S} & \text{are M} \\
\hline
\mathbf{D} & \mathbf{U} \\
\text{All S} & \text{are P}
\end{array}
$$

The final step is to apply the rules of validity to the argument. What these are we shall see in a moment.

6. THE RULES OF VALIDITY

At the beginning of this chapter we described in general terms the conditions of validity that any argument or piece of reasoning must conform to. They must contain a certain internal connection or identity that makes it impossible for one to be true and the other false. For example, given that all men are mortal, it is impossible for Socrates to be a man and not at the same time be mortal. This teaches us that inferences are valid and the relation of implication is well grounded when the identity asserted by the premises is real. The rules of validity attempt to define the precise conditions of this identity by telling us when we can be certain it exists and when we cannot.

For an argument to be valid, it must adhere to the rules of validity. If it violates any one of them, it will be invalid. None of these rules individually accounts for all of the conditions of validity—it takes all of them. Together they clarify the nature of validity and what precisely justifies us in inferring from two propositions a third one.

The following five rules concisely summarize these conditions of validity:

1) **The middle term must be distributed at least once.**
2) **If a term is distributed in the conclusion, it must be distributed in the premise.**
3) **From two negative premises no conclusion follows.**
4) **If one premise is negative, the conclusion must be negative; if the conclusion is negative, one premise must be negative.**
5) **If a syllogism is to be valid, it can have only three terms.**

Let us now examine each of these rules in turn.

1) The first rule states that "for a syllogism to be valid the middle term must be distributed at least once." The rule does not state that the middle term must be distributed *exactly* once; it says it must be distributed *at least* once. In other words, it is not a breach of this rule for the middle term to be distributed in each of the premises of the syllogism.

The reason why the middle term must be distributed at least once is that the two terms of the conclusion are related to each other through the middle term in the premises. If all of the members of the class named by the middle term are not related to some or all of the members of one of the other classes, then it is possible that the major and minor classes may be related to different members of the class named by the middle term, and consequently may not be related to each other at all. For example, from "All dogs are animals" and "All cats are animals," it does not follow that "All dogs are cats," since dogs are one kind of animal and cats are another. Nor does it follow that, because black is a color and white is a color, black is white. It doesn't so follow because black and white are not related in the premises and therefore cannot be related in the conclusion.

This first rule teaches us that the entire middle class must be dealt with in at least one of the premises. Otherwise there would be no way of knowing whether the two premises were referring to the same or to different parts of their connecting middle term, and therefore we would have no assurance that the premises were connected.

Applying this rule immediately invalidates the argument concerning socialists and communists, since, from the statement that all communists are socialists, it does not follow that these socialists are communists. The people concerned may be one kind of socialist, and communists another kind of socialist altogether.

Syllogisms whose middle term is undistributed commit the *fallacy of undistributed middle.*

2) The second rule states that "If a term is distributed in the conclusion, it must be distributed in the premise." This prohibits passage from an undistributed term in the premises to a distributed term in the conclusion. That is, it prohibits passage from "some" in the premises to "all" in the conclusion. It does not prohibit passage from a distributed term in the premises ("all") to an undistributed term in the conclusion ("some"). The rule tells us that if a term is undistributed in its premise, it cannot be distributed in the conclusion, although it is possible that a term may be distributed in its premise but undistributed in the conclusion. The underlying principle here is that you cannot logically conclude with more than you begin with but you may conclude with less.

As an example of the violation of this rule, let us take the following argument:

> Nothing emotional is truthful because of the following reasons: Much propaganda is not truthful, and all propaganda is emotional.

Submitting this argument to syllogistic analysis, we find:

A. The conclusion is, "Nothing emotional is truthful."

B. The major premise is, "Much propaganda is not truthful" (the proposition, that is, having as its terms the middle term "propaganda" and the predicate term "truthful").

C. The minor premise is "All propaganda is emotional" (the proposition, that is, having as its terms the middle term "propaganda" and the subject term "emotional").

D. Put into proper class-analysis form and symbolized, we obtain the following syllogism:

M   **P**

Some (propaganda) is not (a thing that is truthful)

M   **S**

All (propaganda) is (a thing that is emotional)

———————————————

S   **P**

No (thing that is emotional) is (truthful)

E. Abstracting its structure and indicating its distribution, we get:

U   **D**

Some M are not P

D   **U**

All M are S

————————

D   **D**

No S are P

We can now apply the rules of validity to the argument, remembering that only if the syllogism passes all the rules of validity can we declare it valid. The first rule states that if a syllogism is to be valid, its middle term must be distributed at least once. Is the latter true? A quick glance indicates that it is. The second rule states that if a term is distributed in the conclusion, it must be distributed in the premise. The P term is distributed in the conclusion and in the premise. The P term, then, does not violate the rule. The S term, however, is also distributed in the conclusion; if this argument is to be valid, that term must be distributed in the premise as well. But it is not. The syllogism therefore breaks down at this point by committing what is known as the *fallacy of illicit minor*— going from "some" in the premise to "all" in the conclusion, which is invalid logically.

Let us consider the following example:

> Of course all communists are socialists, but I need hardly remind you that many people are not communists. It follows that at least some people are not socialists.

Following the procedure just outlined, we note that:

a. The conclusion of this syllogism is, "Some people are not socialists."
b. The major premise is, "All communists are socialists."
c. The minor premise is, "Some people are not communists."
d. Put in proper logical form and symbolized, we get:

```
        M                 P
All (communists) are (socialists)
        S                 M
Some (people) are not (communists)
```

```
        S                 P
Some (people) are not (socialists)
```

e. Abstracting its structure and putting in its distribution, we get:

```
      D      U
All M are  P
           U        D
Some  S  are not  M
```

```
      U        D
Some  S  are not  P
```

Again we need to apply the rules of validity to the argument. We note first that it does not violate the first rule since the middle term is distributed twice. (This is not a violation of the rule, which states that the middle term must be distributed *at least once*.) Secondly, although the minor term is not distributed in the conclusion (and hence the second rule does not apply to it), the major term is distributed there. If this argument is to be valid, the major term will also have to be distributed in the premise. As we see, it is not. Since the violation involves the major term, this fallacy is called the *fallacy of illicit major*. That is, the syllogism goes from information about only some of the members of the major term to conclude something regarding all of them. What applies to some, however, may not apply to all, and we have no logical warrant to conclude that it does.

Syllogisms are composed of propositions, and, like their components, are characterized and specified by two main features—namely, their *quantity* and *quality*. The first two rules of validity deal with quantity. The next two rules concern violations involving a syllogism's quality.

3) The third rule states that from two negative premises no valid conclusion follows. In other words, for a syllogism to be valid, at least one premise must be affirmative in quality. Let us see why this must be so. If both premises were negative, S and P would be entirely unrelated to the middle term, and if each is unrelated to the middle term, how could we know they are related to each other? With both premises in the negative, we in effect have no middle term and know only that two terms are each different from a third. Thus, we do not have any way to judge how the two are related to each other, if indeed they are related at all. This is why the fallacy that arises from the violation of this rule is sometimes called the *fallacy of exclusive premises* or, more commonly, the *fallacy of two negative premises*.

Though convincing instances of this type of fallacious syllogism are rare, since we don't often make this kind of mistake, the following, would be an example of it:

> Since no civil servant is entitled to vote, and since none of these men are civil servants, it follows that all of these men are entitled to vote.

Put into proper class-analysis form and symbolized, we obtain the following syllogism:

M   P
No (civil servant) is (entitled to vote)
S   M
None (of these men) is (a civil servant)
_____
S   P
All (of these men) are (entitled to vote)

Abstracting its structure and indicating its distribution, we get:

D   **D**
No M is P
D   **D**
No S is M
_____
D   **U**
All S is P

Going through the rules of validity, we discover that although this syllogism passes the first two rules (involving quantity), it breaches the third rule (involving quality).

Maybe it was immediately apparent to you that this argument violates the third rule, even before we took the trouble to write it out and symbolize it. The application of this rule requires some care, however, for some arguments will appear to breach it without really doing so. Consider, for instance, the following example:

> No drug addicts are fully trustworthy people, for no drug addicts are normal and no abnormal person is fully trustworthy.

Submitting this argument to syllogistic analysis, we find:

a. The conclusion is "No drug addicts are fully trustworthy people."
b. The major premise is "No abnormal persons are fully trustworthy people."
c. The minor premise is "No drug addicts are normal persons."
d. Put into proper class-analysis form and symbolized, we get the following syllogism:

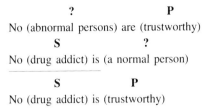

$$? \qquad\qquad P$$
No (abnormal persons) are (trustworthy)
$$S \qquad\qquad\qquad ?$$
No (drug addict) is (a normal person)

$$S \qquad\qquad P$$
No (drug addict) is (trustworthy)

As the question marks indicate, we cannot quite complete this fourth step, since the syllogism has two different middle terms. In addition, the argument breaches the third rule, since it has two negative premises. We might be tempted, therefore, to declare this argument invalid, since it seems to violate two separate rules. But the argument only seems invalid; it is in fact valid. The argument only verbally appears to contain too many terms and two negative premises; by applying to it one of the logical equivalences we learned in the last chapter, we can clarify its true structure.

Since this argument has to get rid of its negative premises if it is to be valid, let us transform the negatives to affirmatives by obversion. By obverting the minor premise, we get rid of one of the negative premises and the extra term, and end up with the following syllogism:

$$M \qquad\qquad\qquad P$$
No (abnormal persons) are (trustworthy)
$$S \qquad\qquad\qquad M$$
All (drug addicts) are (abnormal persons)

$$S \qquad\qquad P$$
No (drug addict) is (trustworthy)

Abstracting its structure and putting in its distribution, we get:

$$D \quad D$$
No M is P
$$D \quad U$$
All S is M

$$D \quad D$$
No S is P

Applying the rules of validity, we find that this syllogism is valid.

You may think that if by applying the logical operations of obversion or contraposition we can transform invalid arguments into valid ones, why not do so in all cases, such as the argument noted previously:

No (civil servant) is (entitled to vote)
None (of these men) are (civil servants)

All (of these men) are (entitled to vote)

It is true that by obverting the minor premise in this argument we can dispose of the negative premises. But doing so gives us the proposition, "All of these men are non-civil servants," resulting in a syllogism with four terms: (1) civil servants, (2) non-civil servants, (3) these men, and (4) entitled to vote.

If we tried to take the converse and then the obverse (of that converse) of the major premise (getting the proposition "All who are entitled to vote are non-civil servants") we could once again get rid of the extra term. But this would result in the following syllogism:

$$\begin{array}{cc} \mathbf{P} & \mathbf{M} \\ \text{All (entitled to vote) are (non-civil servants)} \\ \mathbf{S} & \mathbf{M} \\ \text{All (of these men) are (non-civil servants)} \\ \hline \mathbf{S} & \mathbf{P} \\ \text{All (of these men) are (entitled to vote)} \end{array}$$

Symbolizing the form of this syllogism, it becomes obvious that it commits the fallacy of undistributed middle:

$$\begin{array}{cc} \mathbf{D} & \mathbf{U} \\ \text{All P is M} \\ \mathbf{D} & \mathbf{U} \\ \text{All S is M} \\ \hline \mathbf{D} & \mathbf{U} \\ \text{All S is P} \end{array}$$

With further work, we could avoid this particular fallacy too. But as you may suspect, it will break another rule and commit still another fallacy. This argument, being structurally faulty to begin with, cannot be saved by any of our logical operations of equivalence. Only when one of the additional terms is the complement (the logical opposite) of one of the other three can these operations help bring its true nature and structure into clearer focus. Such arguments, as in the drug addict example, will arouse suspicion because they will generally have more than one fault, such as too many terms or two negative premises. These faults can cancel each other out by way of these logical operations.

4) The fourth rule, like the third, concerns quality of premises. It states that if one premise is negative the conclusion must be negative, and that if the conclusion is negative one premise must be negative.

We seldom violate this rule, which we can recognize intuitively. When one term is asserted to belong to the middle term, and one denied as belonging to it (as happens when one premise is affirmative and the other negative) the only conclusion is that they have no relation to each other. That is, it is a syllogism with a negative conclusion. We seem to realize intuitively that if one premise is negative we have excluded one of the terms from the middle term, and this prevents our deducing anything about the relation of S and P except that they are in some way excluded from each other.

The fallacies that result when this rule is broken are sometimes called the *fallacy of a negative premise without a negative conclusion* and the *fallacy of a negative conclusion without a negative premise.* The latter is also sometimes called the *fallacy of drawing a negative conclusion from affirmative premises.* The following argument would be an example of this fallacy:

"All sculpture is fascinating, but since some golden things are not fascinating, it follows that some golden things are pieces of sculpture."

Put in class-analysis form and symbolized, this argument reads:

    P   M
All (sculpture) is (a thing that fascinates)
    S   M
Some (golden things) are not (things that fascinate)
    _____
    S   P
Some (golden things) are (pieces of sculpture)

Since the S term ("golden things") is excluded in this argument from the M term ("things that fascinate"), we have no way of telling how and if it is related to the P term ("sculpture"). If two terms (S and P) agree with each other, they must stand in the same relation to a third term (M). But if the S and P, as in this syllogism, are not related to M in the same way in the premises, then they cannot be in agreement with one another in the conclusion.

5) The fifth rule states that if a syllogism is to be valid, it can have only three terms. A syllogism that contains more than three terms is said to commit the *fallacy of four terms* or the *fallacy of too many terms* (if it has more than four). If it has four terms because one of them is used equivocally (in one sense in its premise and in a different sense in the conclusion), it commits the *fallacy of equivocation.*

This rule can be broken in two ways: (1) when the argument explicitly makes use of four terms, and (2) when we seem to have three terms verbally but, because of some ambiguity in the meaning of one of the terms, there are really four logically distinct terms.

The following is an example of an argument breaking this rule in the first way:

Some cooks are taxidermists because some cooks stuff turkeys, and anyone who stuffs animals is a taxidermist.

Setting this argument out in proper class-analysis form, we get the following syllogism:

> All (who stuff animals) are (taxidermists)
> Some (cooks) are (people who stuff turkeys)
> _____
> Some (cooks) are (taxidermists)

Although "stuff animals" and "stuff turkeys" may appear similar and therefore be easily confused, in this context they represent widely different notions. This argument therefore contains four terms and is consequently invalid.

The following is a more difficult and subtle example of such a four-term argument:

> No one is free who is in bondage to another, and no lover can say he is not in bondage to his or her beloved. Therefore, no lover is free.

We have in this argument the following terms: (1) lover, (2) free, (3) in bondage to another, and (4) in bondage to his or her beloved. Here again it may be easy to overlook the difference between being enslaved in the ordinary way ("in bondage to another") and being enraptured ("in bondage to his or her beloved"). But the difference is great enough to make the conclusion highly suspect.

Examples such as these, involving the explicit yet subtle use of four terms, should be distinguished from those containing only three terms, as in the following example:

> Only man is rational; but since no woman is a man, it follows that no woman is rational.

This argument, if one may call it such, appears to have only three terms, but because one of them ("man") is used in two different senses, it in effect has four: (1) woman, (2) rational, (3) man/male, and (4) man/human being.

Here is another example of an argument that appears to have three terms but in effect has four:

> Men who are not able to master their lower self are not strong men. Since professional boxers are all strong men, they are able to master this aspect of their psyche.

This argument equivocates, since the term "strong" is used in a physical sense in the premise but in a psychological sense in the conclusion. Professional boxers may be very strong in the ring but far less so in everyday life.

If you detect such a possible shift in meaning, the argument need not be analyzed further; it will be a case of the fallacy of equivocation. It is sufficient simply to identify the term involved and to explain briefly the nature of the shift.

7. TWO ADDITIONAL RULES OF VALIDITY

The first states that ''from two particular premises no conclusion follows''; the second states that ''if one premise is particular, the conclusion must be particular.''

But these two rules are superfluous, for they are only violated if one of the five rules above has already been violated. Nevertheless they are useful, for they represent a quick and practical way of recognizing that a syllogism is invalid. Consider the following example:

> Some dictatorships are unstable, but since some governments are not dictatorships, it follows that some governments are not unstable.

Remembering these additional rules enables us to recognize immediately that this argument, based as it is on two particular premises, is invalid. It would take considerably more time to do this using only the five other traditional rules.

Nevertheless the additional rule covering the example is theoretically superfluous. Putting the argument in proper logical form will demonstrate that it commits the fallacy of illicit major:

M	P		U U
Some (dictatorships) are (unstable)			Some M is P
S	**M**		U D
Some (governments) are not (dictatorships)			Some S is not M
S	**P**		U D
Some (governments) are not (unstable)			Some S is not P

The major term, as we see, is distributed in the conclusion but not in the premise.

But if a syllogism breaks one of these two rules, we needn't resort to actual examples to prove whether or not it breaks one of the other rules. We can simply and systematically consider all the possibilities and see whether or not this is so.

Regarding the first of these two additional rules (namely, that from two particular premises no conclusion follows), the following are the only possible combinations:

$$I \quad O \quad I \quad O$$
$$I \quad O \quad O \quad I$$

And of these possible combinations:

1. **II** does not distribute the middle term, and therefore would commit the fallacy of undistributed middle.
2. **OO** would commit the fallacy of two negative premises.

3. **IO or OI** would require that the conclusion be negative (according to rule 4). However, a negative conclusion means that (as a minimum in the case of an O) the major term must be distributed in the major premise. But neither IO nor OI can distribute more than one term. Hence an argument having two negative premises will be invalid because it will commit either the fallacy of illicit major or that of undistributed middle. Of course, matters will be worse if the conclusion is an E, for then, to avoid the fallacies of illicit major or illicit minor, three terms would need to be distributed in the premises (the third to avoid the fallacy of undistributed middle). But a combination such as IO or OI can distribute a total of only one term between them.

Regarding the second of these additional rules—"If one premise is particular, the conclusion must be particular"—the following are the only possible combinations:

$$A \quad I \quad E \quad I \quad A \quad O \quad E \quad O$$
$$I \quad A \quad I \quad E \quad O \quad A \quad O \quad E$$

Since the order of the premises does not matter, the combinations are reducible to four:

$$E \quad A \quad E \quad A$$
$$O \quad I \quad I \quad O$$

And of these possible combinations:

1. **EO** commits the fallacy of two negative premises.
2. **AI** would permit only an A conclusion, since it contains only affirmatives. Since an A distributes its subject term, this means a total of two terms would need to be distributed in the premises to avoid illicit minor and undistributed middle. However, the AI distributes only one term. If that term is the middle, this combination will result in the fallacy of illicit minor; if that term is the minor term, it will result in the fallacy of undistributed middle.
3. **EI or AO** would require as a minimum a negative conclusion to allow them to be considered premises, since each contains a negative premise. An E conclusion, however, would distribute both its subject and predicate terms. Therefore, to avoid either illicit minor or illicit major (and undistributed middle), a total of three terms would have to be distributed in the premises. But EI and AO distribute only a total of two each and therefore will invariably commit one or the other of these three different fallacies, if the conclusion is other than a particular negative (O).

These, then, are the rules governing validity in syllogistic reasoning.

8. DICTUM DE OMNE ET NULLO

Can we reduce these rules to a single principle of reasoning, one that will summarize its very nature and essence? Aristotle thought that there was such a principle. In its Latin form, it is known as the *dictum de omne et nullo,* which can be understood as "Whatever is true of all is true of each, and whatever is true of none is false of each."

For Aristotle this was the only self-evident principle of logic and the only true and secure basis for logical deduction. Certainty can be achieved, he thought, only under its conditions. These alone marked the limits of validity; anything less was always liable to error.

Stating this as the basic principle of reasoning, Aristotle assumed that all valid inference is expressible in syllogistic form, and that all syllogistic inference should conform to the first-figure syllogism, exemplified in the classic example:

> All men are mortal
> Socrates is a man
> _____
> Socrates is mortal

Some logicians question Aristotle's assumptions, believing that it is neither possible nor desirable to attempt to reduce all reasoning to the first-figure syllogism. They believe that there are interesting varieties of thought not capable of being expressed syllogistically, let alone by way of the first figure. Others have accepted it, if not as an exhaustive account of reasoning, certainly as a model or standard against which all reasoning should be evaluated. There are other kinds of reasoning, including some not easily expressed or reducible syllogistically. Nevertheless, if our aim is logical certainty and validity, we can have no better exemplar than the classic syllogism. Anything less cannot lay claim to the notion of absolute certainty expressed by the concept of validity.

9. COMPLICATIONS

The examples used to illustrate the rules of validity were both simplified and abbreviated, for their purpose was mainly to illustrate the rules and not the difficulties one may encounter in dealing with actual, typical examples. We turn now to more challenging cases.

Ordinary speech, as we noted in the last chapter, is marked by the use of such linguistic devices as "only" and "none but," the opposition of such phrases as "few" and "a few," and the use of multiple negations and convoluted expressions. All these need to be kept in mind, and, where they appear, to be accounted for and appropriately accommodated.

To begin with, let us consider the following example:

> Only intelligent persons are eligible to attend a university. Since Jones is intelligent, we know she is eligible.

Although this example is still highly abbreviated, it presents certain difficulties. The major premise ("Only intelligent persons are eligible to attend a university'') begins with ''only,'' which cannot simply be dropped but needs to be accounted for. We have a choice of either translating it into an A proposition, remembering to reverse its subject and predicate terms (''All eligible to attend university are intelligent''), or into an E proposition, with the subject negated (''No one who is not intelligent is eligible to attend university''). Since the rest of the argument consists of affirmative propositions, we would only complicate matters by translating this first proposition into the universal negative. Therefore the A would be a better choice. The second difficulty posed by this example is that it makes use of a singular subject (''Jones'') in the minor premise which can only be treated as a universal (''All Jones is intelligent''). Finally, we have to realize that the pronoun ''she'' in the conclusion (''we know she is eligible'') refers back to Jones and will need to be translated as such (''All Jones is eligible'').

Put in proper logical form, this argument will now read:

$$
\begin{array}{cc}
\mathbf{P} & \mathbf{M} \\
\text{All (eligible) are (intelligent)} \\
\mathbf{S} & \mathbf{M} \\
\text{All (Jones) is (intelligent)} \\
\hline
\mathbf{S} & \mathbf{P} \\
\text{All (Jones) is (eligible)}
\end{array}
$$

A glance at the terms will let us know immediately that this argument, in which both middle terms fall on the predicate side of A propositions, commits the fallacy of undistributed middle. Recognizing this is easy; what may be difficult is deciding which of the statements is the conclusion. As stated before, where this is not made clear by such terms as ''therefore,'' ''hence,'' or ''consequently,'' the conclusion must be determined by ascertaining the main thrust of the argument, and by a process of elimination. (The proposition ''since Jones is intelligent'' is obviously not the conclusion.)

Let us now consider another sort of difficulty, represented by the following example:

> Only the unafraid are unprepared. Jones is obviously fearful, so we know she is prepared.

There is no difficulty about deciding which is the conclusion of this argument—it is obviously the statement beginning with ''so.'' The conclusion is also one of the two relatively less complicated propositions of the argument. Establishing that will provide us with two of the three terms of the syllogism. Thus we have as our conclusion ''she'' representing the antecedent ''Jones'':

$$
\overline{}
$$
All (Jones) is (prepared)

Since the proposition "Jones is obviously fearful" is the next simplest proposition, let us turn to it. Containing the minor term "Jones," it therefore represents the minor premise. We now have as our emerging syllogism:

> All (Jones) is (fearful)
> ───────────────────
> All (Jones) is (prepared)

The next step is to deal with the major premise, "Only the unafraid are unprepared." First we deal with the word "only." Since the remaining propositions of this argument are in the affirmative, we would normally translate it with the A proposition. Thus we get the proposition "All unprepared are unafraid." Adding this to what we have derived so far, we get the following result:

> All (unprepared) are (unafraid)
> All (Jones) is (fearful)
> ───────────────────
> All (Jones) is (prepared)

We obviously have too many terms. However, "fearful" and "afraid" (in "unafraid") are closely related terms, and therefore no harm will be done if we change "fearful" to "afraid." Our syllogism will now read:

> All (unprepared) are (unafraid)
> All (Jones) is (afraid)
> ───────────────────
> All (Jones) is (prepared)

We still have two extra terms, which we could dispose of by getting rid of the *un*'s attached to the terms "prepared" and "afraid." The logical operation that will enable us to change these negations is contraposition. Taking the contrapositive of "All unprepared are unafraid," we get "All afraid are prepared." Substituting this equivalent proposition for the original one, we now get the following syllogism:

>   **M**   **P**
> All (afraid) are (prepared)
>   **S**   **M**
> All (Jones) is (afraid)
> ───────────────────
>   **S**   **P**
> All (Jones) is (prepared)

Applying the rules of validity to this syllogism, we will find that the following is valid:

D U
All M is P
D U
All S is M

D U
All S is P

As our final example, we present an argument that requires for its resolution another piece of logical information:

> It is false that some apologies can rectify an error. And it is also not the case that some apologies are not half-hearted measures. Consequently, it must be the case that no half-hearted measures can rectify an error.

As in the previous case, the conclusion seems the clearest and easiest of the three propositions to deal with, so let us begin with it:

No (half-hearted measures) are (things that can rectify an error)

But what can we do with the statements that begin "It is false . . ." and "It is not the case that . . ."? These phrases deny that what follows them is true. What follows the first phrase is an I proposition ("some apologies are things that can rectify an error"); what follows the second phrase is an O proposition ("some apologies are not half-hearted measures"). Therefore, we can replace each entire proposition with its contradictory. As the square of opposition will help us recall, the contradictory of the I is the E, and the contradictory of the O is the A.

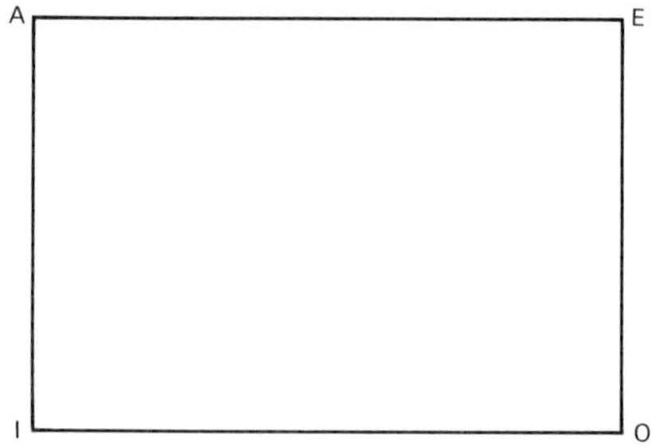

Therefore the major premise of the argument, which asserted that "It is false that some apologies can rectify an error," becomes "No apologies can rectify an error." The minor premise, which asserted that "It is also not the case that some apologies are not half-hearted measures," becomes "All apologies are half-hearted measures."

Incorporating these changes into our syllogism, we get the following result:

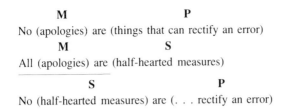

| M | P |
| No (apologies) are (things that can rectify an error) |

Applying the rules of validity to this argument, we find that despite all this effort the argument turns out to be invalid, committing the fallacy of illicit minor.

10. TESTING SYLLOGISMS BY VENN DIAGRAMS

The rules of the syllogism clarify the nature of arguments and help us understand why certain conclusions can be inferred from certain premises and others cannot. For further clarification, the Venn diagrams can be helpful.

Venn diagrams are not simply visual illustrations of an argument whose nature has been clarified by the rules of validity. On the contrary, they also show us in a striking way which conclusions follow from given premises and which do not, and clarify the nature of validity and the reasoning process as a whole.

In a valid argument the conclusion necessarily follows from the premises. This means that if we grant the truth of the premises we *must* grant the truth of the conclusion. In an invalid argument a conclusion is not necessitated in this way. If in a given argument we can draw circles so that the premises can be shown to be true without showing that the conclusion must be true, then these premises do not necessitate the conclusion. On the other hand, where it is impossible to draw circles which show the premises to be true without showing the conclusion to be true, we know we have a valid argument. Thus, it is possible to diagram the argument.

> All P is M
> All S is M
> ―――――――
> All S is P

in such a way as to show that the premises do not necessitate the conclusion, as follows:

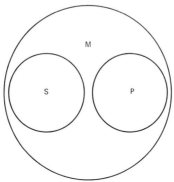

But it would not be possible to do so with the argument

All M is P

All S is M

———————

All S is P

as the following diagram makes obvious:

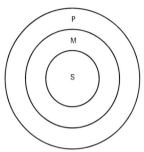

The technique that Venn developed differs from these examples in using overlapping or intersecting circles, as shown in the following diagram:

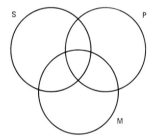

The upper circle on the left always stands for the minor term, the upper circle on the right stands for the major term, and the bottom circle stands for the middle term. Therefore our classic syllogism

M   P

All (men) are (mortal)

S   M

All (Socrates) is (a man)

————————————

S   P

All (Socrates) is (mortal)

All M is P

All S is M

———————

All S is P

would be diagrammed in the following way: Beginning with the three blank intersecting circles (which must be large enough for the work required) we would first record the information given in the major premise. Since the diagram says that all the M's are P's we must shade out that area of the M circle that is not P:

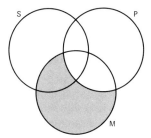

We then go on to add to this information given in the minor premise—that all S's are M's—shading out that area of the S circle that is not M:

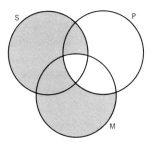

The conclusion of this syllogism, if valid, should now appear without any further diagramming; if it doesn't, the syllogism is not valid. The conclusion of our syllogism is that all the S's are P's; if we look at our final diagram again, we will note that it shows this. This syllogism is therefore valid; the premises as given entail or contain the conclusion inferred.

For further practice in applying this technique, let us take the following syllogism:

No P is M
All S is M
―――――――――
No S is P

Diagramming the major premise of our syllogism, we obtain the following:

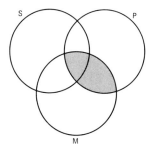

Completing the diagram by entering the information of the minor premise, we get:

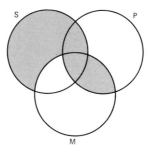

The conclusion states that not a single S is a P—that the area where S and P overlap is empty. The last diagram reveals that this area is empty, and consequently the argument is valid.

To take an example involving a particular premise, let us apply the Venn diagram technique to this syllogism:

> All M is P
> Some S is M
> ---
> Some S is P

When one premise is universal and the other particular, we always diagram the universal first. In this case, we obtain the following result:

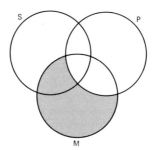

Adding the information given in the minor premise, we obtain the following:

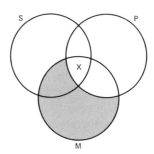

The conclusion of this argument states that some S's are P's, and the diagram shows this to be so.

Let us now take some examples of invalid syllogisms. The following example violates rule 1 and, as a result, commits the fallacy of undistributed middle:

>   All P are M
>   All S are M
>   _____
>   All S are P

Entering the information contained in the premises, and numbering the separate sections for easier identification, we get the following result:

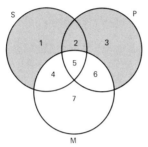

Does our diagram verify that all the S's are P's, as the conclusion asserts? We can see that it does not. It shows that there may be S's that are P's (5), and that there may be S's that are not P's (4). This argument is therefore invalid.

The following syllogism commits the fallacy of illicit minor:

>   All M are P
>   All M are S
>   _____
>   All S are P

Entering the information of both premises, we get the following results:

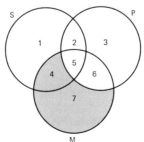

The conclusion states that all the S's are P's. However, the diagram reveals that there might be S's that are not P's, namely in area 1. Thus, this argument too is invalid.

As an example of the fallacy of illicit major, consider the following syllogism:

> All M are P
> No S are M
> _____
> No S are P

Diagramming it, we get the following:

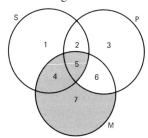

Though the conclusion of the syllogism asserts that not a single S is a P, the diagram shows that there may be some S's that are P's (area 2). This syllogism is therefore invalid.

Turning to the fallacies concerning quality, let us consider first the following syllogism, which commits the fallacy of two negative premises:

> No M are P
> No S are M
> _____
> All S are P

Diagramming this syllogism, we get the following result:

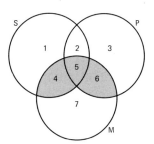

The conclusion asserts that all the S's are P's. The diagram, however, shows that there may be S's (in area 1) that are not P's. The syllogism is therefore invalid.

Finally, let us take the following example of a syllogism that commits the fallacy of drawing a negative conclusion from two affirmative premises:

> All M are P
> Some S are M
> _____
> Some S are not P

Diagramming this syllogism, we obtain the following result:

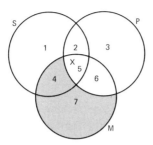

The conclusion of the syllogism asserts that some S's are not P's, but the diagram does not show an X in area 1, and none may be there. This conclusion thus cannot be said to follow with certainty from these premises.

The diagramming of syllogisms with particular propositions may entail certain difficulties. We have already seen that, in cases of syllogisms composed of a universal and a particular premise, the universal is always diagrammed first. This is because the universal compartments are always shaded, which enables us to place the X in the exact compartment that contains members. Were we to plot the particular premise first, we would have a choice of two areas in which to insert the X without knowing precisely where it belongs. In the case of the syllogism

> Some P are M
> All M are S
> _____
> Some S are P

if we tried to plot the particular premise first, we would not know whether to place the X in compartment 5 or 6:

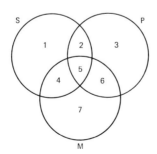

However, if we plot the major premise first, this eliminates 6 as a possibility, leaving compartment 5 as the only area where X can be placed:

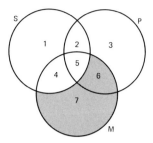

If we diagram the universal first and there still remains some ambiguity as to where to place the X, then it should be placed on the line that separates the two compartments, as follows:

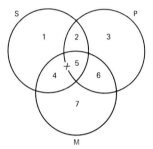

but never either outside of the diagram altogether, as in this example:

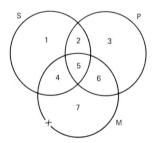

or on the intersection of two lines:

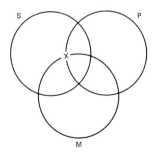

Let us look at another example:

> Some M are P
> All S are M
> _____
> Some S are P

After diagramming the universal premise, as follows:

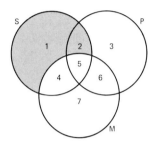

we are left in doubt whether to put the X of the particular premise (in this case the major premise) in area 5 or 6; we are therefore forced to place it on the arc separating the two compartments. Though the conclusion states that there definitely are some S's that are P's, this is not shown by the diagram.

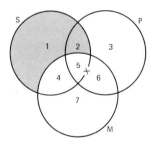

The X on the boundary may in reality belong to area 6 rather than area 5. Not being sure that it belongs to area 5, we cannot say that this conclusion follows validly from these premises. (From the rules of validity, we know that this syllogism commits the fallacy of undistributed middle.)

Let us consider another such example:

> All M are P
> Some S are not M
> _____
> Some S are not P

Diagramming the universal premise first, we get:

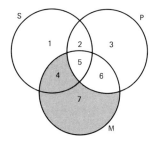

When we diagram the particular premise, we aren't sure where to put the X. Shall we put it in area 1 or area 2? Not being able to decide, we place it on the arc separating these two areas:

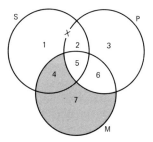

But this means that the conclusion, which states that there are S's that are not P's, is similarly doubtful, since we do not know which area the X's really occupy.

Venn diagrams provide us with a striking visual representation of syllogistic reasoning. Although they cannot tell us *why* certain syllogisms are valid and others are not, the clarification they lend to the reasoning process enables us to see more exactly why our conclusions are valid or invalid. For this reason, they are extremely useful aids in the detection and understanding of fallacy.

The procedures for using Venn diagrams must be adhered to strictly. These are relatively simple and may be summarized briefly:

1. Always follow a consistent pattern in setting up the diagrams. If you acquire the habit of using the upper left circle to represent the minor term, do so always. And similarly with the remaining terms.
2. Make the circles large enough to enter the required information without crowding.
3. Only the major and minor premises of the syllogism are diagrammed. If the syllogism is valid, the diagram of the conclusion will be contained in the diagram of the premises.
4. If a premise asserts that a particular class is empty, the area of the diagram representing that class is shaded.
5. Mark with an X the diagram area that represents a class that contains at least one member.
6. Always shade the universal premise before plotting the particular.

7. When a proposition does not specify where the X is to be placed, place it on the line separating the two sections.

11. EXISTENTIAL IMPORT

The examples of syllogisms that we have considered up to this point have been unaffected by the question of existential import. Their validity wasn't influenced by whether or not the members designated by their classes in the propositions making up the syllogisms exist or not. Of the 256 different syllogisms, however, there are 9 that are so affected (leaving only 15 of the 24 that are unconditionally valid). Venn diagrams, designed on the basis of the nonexistential implication of universal propositions, fail to show the validity of these syllogisms.

As an example of these nine, let us consider the following syllogism:

> All M are P
> All M are S
> _____
> Some S are P

This syllogism passes all the rules of validity: The middle term is distributed at least once; rule 2 does not apply to it, since neither its minor nor its major term is distributed in the conclusion; the rules of quality don't apply to it, since its premises and conclusion are all in the affirmative. But when we represent this syllogism with a Venn diagram, it shows the syllogism to be invalid:

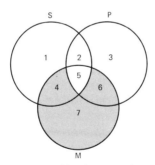

The conclusion states that there are S's that are P's; the diagram does not show this, since no X appears in area 5.

But Venn diagrams may accommodate these nine syllogisms, by recording that the subjects of the universal premises denote existing things, and placing an X in the appropriate area. In diagramming the syllogism mentioned, for example, we would shade out areas 4 and 7 and enter a circled X on the arc separating areas 5 and 6. (The X is circled to indicate that it is based on a special assumption regarding universal propositions.)

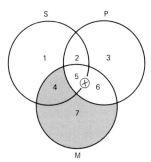

Located where it is, the circled X tells us that we do not know whether these X's are to be found in area 5 or area 6. This is clarified when we enter the information provided by the minor premise, which requires that we shade out area 6, leaving area 5 as the only place where these X's are to be found:

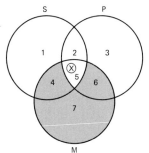

Let us take as a further example the following syllogism:

>   All P are M
>   No S are M
>   ――――――――――
>   Some S are not P

This syllogism could have concluded with an E proposition and would have been equally valid. Had it concluded with an E proposition, as follows:

>   All P are M
>   No S are M
>   ――――――――――
>   No S are P

a Venn diagram would also have shown it to be valid:

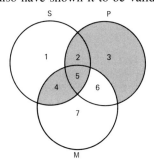

The major premise would shade out areas 2 and 3, and the minor premise would shade out areas 4 and 5. The conclusion tells us that the result is that areas 2 and 5 are empty (shaded).

However, the original conclusion stated that after recording the information provided by the two premises, we should find an X in area 1, but there is no X there. We can reconcile these differences by forcing the Venn diagrams to adopt the standpoint of existential import. In the case of this particular syllogism, this would mean entering a circled X in area 1 (in addition to shading out areas 4 and 5) when recording the information provided by the minor premise ("No S are M"). This ensures that we would find an X where the conclusion says it should be (assuming the syllogism is valid).

SUMMARY

Whereas Chapter Two covered immediate inference, the present chapter has looked at mediate inference, inference that requires the help of a third, mediating premise.

Logic achieved its first insight into the nature of inference by the discovery of the structure of the syllogism. The syllogism is a simple case of mediate inference and a valuable tool for logical analysis, because it exhibits a typical form of internal connection that alone is the basis for valid inference.

The categorical syllogism derives its name from the fact that each of the premises, as well as the conclusion, is a categorical proposition. It may be defined as a form of argument consisting of three categorical propositions (two being premises and the third a conclusion drawn from these premises) which contain between them three and only three terms. A syllogistic inference is a comparison of the relations between each of these two terms and the third, in order to discover the relation of the two terms to each other.

In analyzing a syllogism into its parts in order to test its validity, it is necessary first to find and identify the various terms. This is done by beginning with the conclusion. The subject of the conclusion is called the *minor term,* and the predicate of the conclusion is called the *major term.* The premise containing the major term is called the *major premise,* and the one that contains the minor term is called the *minor premise.* Since the premises—one of which gives us information about the conclusion's subject, while the other gives information about its predicate—are logically joined, they must have one term in common. That *middle term* is found in each of the premises, tying the syllogism together and determining whether the conclusion follows from the combination of these premises.

Syllogisms may be further classified by the quantity and quality of the premises and the conclusion, and by the position of the middle term in the premises. The quantity and quality (A, E, I, O) of propositions determine the *mood* of the syllogism; the position of the middle term within the premises determines the *figure* of the syllogism. Mood and figure together give us the *form* of the syllogism, which is expressed by placing the number of its figure after the letters that state its mood—for example, AAA–1.

To determine their formal validity, we must express categorical syllogisms in proper logical form. This involves the following steps: (1) finding the conclusion of the argument; (2) rewriting the argument if necessary, putting the conclusion last; (3) expressing each of its propositions in class-analysis form; (4) identifying the major, minor, and middle terms by use of the symbols P, S, and M; (5) symbolizing the form of the argument; and (6) writing in its distribution. The final step is to apply the rules of validity to the argument, remembering that if an argument violates even one of the rules it will be invalid. Only if it passes *all* the conditions can it be accepted as valid.

The five rules which summarize the most important conditions of validity are the following:

1. The middle term must be distributed at least once.
2. If a term is distributed in the conclusion, it must be distributed in the premise.
3. From two negative premises no conclusion follows.
4. If one premise is negative, the conclusion must be negative; if the conclusion is negative, one premise must be negative.
5. If a syllogism is to be valid, it can have only three terms.

Two other rules are usually given in the traditional list. The first states that "From two particular premises, no conclusion follows"; the second states that "If one premise is particular, the conclusion is particular." But these two rules are really superfluous, because they are violated only if one of the other rules has already been violated.

The violation of rule 1 leads to the *fallacy of the undistributed middle*. The violation of rule 2 leads to either the *fallacy of illicit major* or the *fallacy of illicit minor,* depending upon which term in the conclusion was not distributed in the premise. The violation of rule 3 leads to the *fallacy of two negative premises.* The violation of rule 4 leads to the *fallacy of negative conclusion but no negative premise* or the *fallacy of negative premise but no negative conclusion.* The violation of rule 5 leads to either the *fallacy of too many terms* or the *fallacy of equivocation,* depending upon whether the argument explicitly contains four or more terms, or does so only implicitly when one or more of its terms is used in more than one sense.

Venn diagrams are a visual technique for illustrating and testing syllogisms. The test procedure consists in transferring the information contained in the premises to the diagram, and then inspecting the diagram to see whether it actually represents the claims of the conclusion. The major premise is diagrammed first and the information of the minor premise is then added (or vice versa, if the major premise is particular and the minor universal). If the syllogism is valid, the conclusion should now appear. The sole exception is a syllogism in which a particular conclusion is drawn from two universal premises. Venn diagrams fail to show the validity of such syllogisms, although they can be revised to enable them to do so.

Exercises

I. What rules are broken by syllogisms composed of the following types of propositions (the first in each case being the major premise and the last the conclusion)? (See answers in appendix.)

   1. EOA
   2. EAA
   3. OEE
   4. III
   5. IAO
   6. AIA

II. Determine what type of valid conclusion can result from the following types of premises (the first being the major premise in each case). (See answers in appendix.)

   7. AI
   8. EI
   9. AA
   10. EA
   11. AO

III. Test the validity of the following syllogisms by the Venn diagram method:

   12. AAA–1
   13. EIO–2
   14. AAE–1
   15. IAI–4
   16. AIA–3

IV. Analyze the following syllogisms. First, rewrite the argument in proper class-analysis form, putting the major premise first and the conclusion last. Then symbolize the form of the argument, indicating the distribution of each term by inserting D and U in the appropriate places. Finally, test each syllogism by the five rules of validity; one violation is sufficient to show that the syllogism is invalid. (See appendix for violations.)

17. No passions endure; hate is a passion; therefore, hate does not endure.

18. Epicureans do not hold that virtue is the chief good, but all true philosophers do hold that it is so; accordingly, Epicureans are not true philosophers.

19. Few pediatricians are specialists in surgery, so few general practitioners are pediatricians, since some general practitioners are not specialists in surgery.

20. Philosophers who are not impractical do exist. But few practical people are thinkers; thus a few philosophers are not thinkers.

21. All Americans are not opposed to armed intervention, since many Americans are unafraid of the risk of atomic war, and no one unafraid of running the risk of atomic war is opposed to armed intervention.

22. All honest moralists are good citizens, for only good citizens practice what they preach, and honest moralists practice what they preach.

23. None but huge things are extinct. It follows, therefore, that some dinosaurs are huge, for only extinct things are dinosaurs.

24. All cats like cream and all kittens are pets; therefore, all kittens like cream.

25. Nothing that waddles is graceful. All ducks waddle. Therefore all ducks are ungraceful.

26. All great men are men with vision. Practically all of us are therefore great, for very few of us are blind.

27. Some pleasures are not praiseworthy; hence, since whatever is not praiseworthy is not virtuous, some pleasures are not virtuous.

28. All sculpture is fascinating, but it is false that all things made of gold fascinate. Hence a few golden objects are pieces of sculpture.

29. It is not the case that some coal-tar derivatives are nourishing foods, because none but coal-tar derivatives are artificial dyes, and only nourishing foods are artificial dyes.

30. Gentlemen, this painting is undoubtedly the work of Paul Cézanne. See how the paint has been laid on layer over layer in thin brush strokes. You know that Cézanne applied his paint that way.

31. No happy people are uninspired by what transcends the reach of our everyday modes of perception, and all those who are unable to appreciate the beauty of nature belong to quite a different class from those who are inspired by what transcends the reach of everyday modes of perception. Hence unhappy people are those who cannot appreciate the beauty of nature.

32. Nothing that is right is wrong. But some turns that I make on the freeway are right turns, and so they are not wrong.

33. Only irresponsible persons give up their jobs without reason. Smith is a responsible person, so we can be sure he will not give up his job without reason.

34. All those who lack culture should take a humanities course; since some philosophers are hardly cultured yet, they should all take such a course.

35. Few pilots are skilled. But since no skilled person is unemployed, then it seems to follow that a few pilots are unemployed.

36. All of the ignorant are not free. Thus, since only free people are brave, it follows that no person is characterized by being both brave and ignorant.

37. None but citizens may vote; therefore, you are a citizen, for you are a voter.

38. No nice girl swears; but Jean, when called to the witness stand, swore. Jean is not, therefore, a nice girl.

39. Only petty people are pernicious. Since no petty person is pretty, it must be that all pernicious people are non-petty.

40. Receiving Federal grants means being subject to governmental interference. We are declining all such help, and therefore we will be free of any governmental interference.

41. It is false that all college graduates are intelligent, since all intelligent people get good jobs, and few college graduates get good jobs.

42. (Robinson Crusoe, upon discovering the footprint in the sand:) This footprint is in the shape and size of a human foot, and since every mark having those qualities is the imprint of a human foot, this mark must be one also.

43. Selfish people are not considerate of the rights of others. Those who play stereos with the windows open are not considerate of the rights of others. Hence we may regard them as selfish.

44. No man is an island unto himself. Since Greenland is an island, we know, by deduction alone, that Greenland is not a man.

45. All persons who are persuaded of the value of traditional education are convinced of the need for some type of discipline, and most people who are so convinced are not profligates. So profligates are not persuaded of the value of traditional education.

46. Impiety is a threat to the safety of the city; Socrates is a threat to the safety of the city; hence Socrates is impious.

47. None but those who are contented with their lot are really happy. But a wise man is contented with his lot, and therefore he is really happy.

48. Husbands are men. It takes plenty of courage to be a man. Therefore husbands have plenty of courage.

49. No well-informed person can fail to be aware of the continued arms race. No one who is aware of the continued arms race can feel complacent about the future. How, then, can any well-intentioned person feel complacent about the future?

50. All nonbelievers are nonthinkers. But since all uninformed people are nonbelievers, we may infer that there are no informed nonthinkers.

FOUR

Condensed Arguments

1. DECIPHERING ARGUMENTS

Once an argument has been reduced to its proper logical or syllogistic form, determining whether it is acceptable or not is relatively easy and straightforward. Up to this point we have concentrated almost entirely on learning how to do this.

We must now turn, however, to the most difficult task of all, learning how to decipher arguments as normally and ordinarily expressed. To some extent we have already been exposed to this when we saw how certain key grammatical terms such as "only," "none but," "few," and "it is false that" can complicate arguments.

In addition to such linguistic forms, arguments are marked by two other characteristics. The first occurs when, for rhetorical or other reasons, we present our arguments in a highly abbreviated form with parts intentionally omitted. The second occurs when, not being sure of what we want to say, we become verbose. In the one case we do not say enough; in the other we say too much. The former is easier to deal with than the latter; it is also ground that has been gone over more carefully. The latter is a problem that has come to be studied only relatively recently. We shall deal with verbosity in Chapter Five. Here we will look at highly condensed or compact arguments, traditionally called *enthymemes*.

2. ENTHYMEMES

It is not always apparent that a lot of our ordinary discourse containing inference proceeds by categorical syllogism. There are two main reasons for this: First, we don't usually express our propositions in the somewhat artificial and unnatural class-analysis form. Second, we don't normally state our arguments fully. We may omit one premise, leaving it to be supplied by the reader or listener, or we may state the premises but leave the reader or listener to draw the conclusion. A syllogism with such a missing component is called an *enthymeme*—from a Greek root meaning "in the mind."

Literature is full of enthymemes. They add charm, compactness, and suggestiveness to our expression. The eight Beatitudes in the Sermon on the Mount are enthymemes; in "Blessed are the meek, for they shall inherit the earth," the premise that "All who inherit the earth are blessed" is omitted.

Enthymemes can also be used for purposes of innuendo. "Yon Cassius has a lean and hungry look; . . . such men are dangerous." Omitted is the inference that Cassius is dangerous. "Every radical I have ever met thinks as you do." What is implied is that you are a radical.

Such remarks are rhetorically more powerful and persuasive when stated enthymematically than when enunciated in complete detail. Often an argument is not spelled out completely because the intent is clear without all the parts being explicitly stated. Many propositions are presumed to be common knowledge, and we needn't repeat what everybody knows. "These are natural foods and therefore good for you." (Omitted: the premise that natural foods are good for you.) "Why be ashamed of a mistake? No one's perfect." (Omitted: the premise that what all people are liable to is not a thing to be ashamed of.)

The use of the enthymeme is obviously a time-saving device. A critical reader, however, will be on the lookout for unstated premises or assumptions, for they may not be at all obvious. The missing premise required to validate the argument may be of dubious truth, and the person arguing may have deliberately omitted it so that we wouldn't examine it critically. If arguers can prevent reflection on the premise, they may succeed in gaining our consent to a false conclusion. In short, parts of arguments may be omitted because the argument seems more plausible when they are concealed.

Enthymemes are said to be of the *first, second,* or *third order,* according to whether the major premise, the minor premise, or the conclusion is lacking.

First-order enthymemes are the most frequent. They occur whenever we give a reason for anything without formulating explicitly the general principle that is involved. "You're so fond of children, you'd make an excellent kindergarten teacher." Left unstated is the general rule, "People who are fond of children make excellent kindergarten teachers." *Second-order enthymemes* omit the minor premise. "You'll make an excellent kindergarten teacher. People who are as fond of children as you are always do, you know." What is left unstated is that you're fond of children. Least frequent are *third-order enthymemes,* where we state the rule (the major premise) and the case falling under it (the minor premise) but leave the result or conclusion to be derived by the reader or listener: "People who are fond of children always make excellent kindergarten teachers, and everyone knows how very fond you are of children."

Since enthymemes are abbreviated syllogisms, they are subject to the same rules as syllogisms. They can be valid or invalid. Merely because we can complete an enthymeme does not mean that it is valid. Let us look at each type of enthymeme and practice locating and evaluating the missing part.

The first step in analyzing enthymemes is to put what we have been given in proper logical form. With the enthymeme, "The people in the line can't get in, for they haven't got tickets," we would first try to determine what type of enthymeme it is. Since it consists of a premise and a conclusion, we recognize quickly that it must be either a first- or a second-order enthymeme. Putting it in proper logical form, we get the following:

S   **M**

All (the people in the line) are (people without tickets)

S   **P**

All (the people in the line) are (people who can't get in)

Set down in this way, it becomes clear that a major premise is missing. Recognizing the structure of the syllogism, we know that this premise must consist of a P term and an M term, in this case the term "people who can't get in" (P) and "people without tickets" (M). Knowing the structure of the syllogism, we also know that if this syllogism is to be valid, that premise must be a universal affirmative one with the middle term falling on the subject side of the proposition. (If it were negative it would commit one of the fallacies of quality, and if it were particular it would result in one of the fallacies of quantity.) For that syllogism to be valid, then, the missing premise must be "People who haven't got tickets can't get in." The argument, fully expressed and written out, would now read:

M   **P**

All (people without tickets) are (people who can't get in)

S   **M**

All (people in the line) are (people without tickets)

S   **P**

All (people in the line) are (people who can't get in)

Symbolizing the form of this argument and applying the rules of validity to it, we find it is indeed a valid syllogism:

D   **U**

All M are P

D   **U**

All S are M

D   **U**

All S are P

The middle term is distributed at least once; the S term is distributed in the conclusion and in the premise. All are affirmative propositions and therefore do not break the rules of quality.

First-order enthymemes lack major premises. These are usually statements of general rules or principles ("All men are mortal"). Second-order enthymemes lack minor premises, which are usually statements of the particular case falling under the rule "Socrates is a man").

Second-order enthymemes, emphasizing the specific case rather than the general rule, are less frequent but sometimes less obvious as well. "Apes are not rational animals, because only men are rational." (Omitted: No man is an ape.) "All alcoholics are short-lived; therefore Jim won't live long." (Omitted: Jim is an alcoholic.) "The Thirty Years' War was long and bitter, like all religious wars." (Omitted: The Thirty Years' War was a religious war.)

The procedure of locating and evaluating second-order enthymemes is the same as for those of the first order. Given the example "Not all starlike bodies are stars, since planets are not stars," we would proceed with what we have:

$$\begin{array}{cc} \textbf{M} & \textbf{P} \end{array}$$
No (planets) are (stars)

$$\begin{array}{cc} \textbf{S} & \textbf{P} \end{array}$$
Some (starlike bodies) are not (stars)

It is clear from this that the enthymeme is missing a minor premise, a proposition consisting of the M term ("planets") and the S term ("starlike bodies"). For this enthymeme to be valid, the missing minor premise would need to be affirmative (otherwise the syllogism would have two negative premises, and from two negative premises no conclusion follows). Using the minimum assumption needed to make the argument valid (not, for example, using an A proposition if an I would do), we would choose as our minor premise the proposition "Some planets are starlike bodies" (I). Fully written out, the syllogism would then read:

$$\begin{array}{cc} \textbf{M} & \textbf{P} \end{array}$$
No (planets) are (stars)
$$\begin{array}{cc} \textbf{S} & \textbf{M} \end{array}$$
Some (starlike bodies) are (planets)

$$\begin{array}{cc} \textbf{S} & \textbf{P} \end{array}$$
Some (starlike bodies) are not (stars)

Symbolizing it and applying the rules of validity, we find that it too is valid.

Had we used an A minor premise instead of an I, this syllogism would also have been valid, but then the proposition, making this larger claim, would have been false (since obviously not all starlike bodies are planets) and the argument would be unsound. We can only make the lesser claim on the author's behalf;

otherwise we may misrepresent what the author might have said had he or she stated the argument fully.

In a third-order enthymeme, both premises are stated, leaving the conclusion to be inferred. This is an effective rhetorical device, because we are likely to take more interest in ideas that we ourselves arrive at than those made explicit by someone else. The following is a famous and oft-quoted remark by the eighteenth-century Scottish philosopher David Hume:

> Our ideas reach no farther than our experience; we have no experience of divine attributes and operations; I need not conclude my syllogism; you can draw the inference yourself.

The inference, of course, is that we can have no ideas of divine attributes and operations—that is, any knowledge of God.

The procedure to follow in making explicit the suppressed or unexpressed component is similar to what we have already used. We begin by putting what we have in proper logical form. For the third-order enthymeme "Cowardice is always contemptible, and this was clearly a case of cowardice," we would obtain the following result:

$$\begin{array}{cc} \textbf{M} & \textbf{P} \\ \text{All (cowardice) are (contemptible)} \\ \textbf{S} & \textbf{M} \\ \text{All (this act) is (cowardice)} \end{array}$$

Knowing that the conclusion of a syllogism is always a combination of the S and P terms, we realize that the implied conclusion of this syllogism is the proposition:

$$\begin{array}{cc} \textbf{S} & \textbf{P} \\ \text{All (this act) is (a contemptible act)} \end{array}$$

which is a classic first-figure syllogism. Symbolizing the structure of this syllogism and applying the rules of validity to it, we find that it is valid.

3. MAKING ENTHYMEMES VALID

As suggested earlier, always try to supply the component that will make the enthymeme valid. Our object is to be true to the speaker's or writer's intention, placing the most favorable interpretation on what was said. This means (1) stating the missing component affirmatively or negatively as required, in order to avoid fallacies of quality; (2) placing the distributed term on the subject or predicate side of the supplied proposition to avoid fallacies of distribution; and (3) using particular propositions instead of universal ones, to avoid supplying suspect premises that will make the syllogism valid but the argument as a whole unsound.

This last situation is very common. Sometimes only the addition of an implausible proposition as premise will make the argument valid, while a plausible proposition makes the argument invalid. Here is a typical example: "He can't possibly have a telephone, since he's not listed in the directory." Rewriting what we have, we obtain the following:

$$\frac{\text{S} \qquad\qquad \text{M}}{\text{No (he) is (listed in the directory)}}$$

$$\text{S} \qquad\qquad\qquad \text{P}$$
$$\text{No (he) is (one who has a telephone)}$$

The enthymeme clearly lacks a major premise. To be valid, this major premise would need to be an affirmative proposition (to avoid the fallacy of two negative premises). The missing premise has to be affirmative and universal, with the predicate term falling on the subject side of the proposition (to avoid the fallacy of illicit major). The only premise that would make this argument valid, then, is

$$\text{P} \qquad\qquad\qquad\qquad \text{M}$$
$$\text{All (those who have telephones) are (listed in the directory).}$$

This obviously makes the argument suspect, for although it is true that all those who are listed have telephones, it is not the case that all those who have telephones are listed.

By making explicit what is only implicit, we can decide not only whether the argument is valid but whether the unstated premise is reliable. If it is not, that is reason enough to reject the argument.

Enthymemes remind us again of the two basic questions that determine whether an argument deserves our assent or not: Are the premises true? and Is the reasoning valid? Only when both questions can be answered affirmatively can an argument compel our assent. Don't allow the compactness of an argument to fool you.

SUMMARY

The meaning and validity of an argument can be difficult to determine if the example is either highly abbreviated or verbose. Incomplete or compact arguments are called *enthymemes,* from the Greek word meaning "in the mind." Enthymemes are of the first, second, or third order according to whether the major premise, the minor premise, or the conclusion is lacking. The unexpressed component may have been intentionally omitted for rhetorical reasons, or because it did not require expression (being either obvious or common knowledge), or indeed for shady reasons.

Enthymemes, being abbreviated syllogisms, are subject to the same rules as syllogisms and may be valid or invalid. Completing an enthymeme does not necessarily make it valid. Although most enthymemes can be made valid, sometimes this is possible only by introducing an implausible or false proposition which makes the argument unsound. We study enthymemes to help us recognize when this is the case.

Exercises

I. Name the order and discuss the correctness of each of the following enthymemes. Write the arguments in standard form, adding a missing premise or conclusion to make the completed argument valid, if possible. Enclose the added proposition in square brackets for easy identification. The first example has been done. (See appendix for orders.)

  1. All that glitters is not gold, so gold is not the only precious metal.

M	P		U	D
Some (glittering things) are not (gold)			Some M are not P	
	S		U	U
Some (glittering things) are (precious metals)			Some M are S	
S	P		U	D
Some (precious metals) are not (gold)			Some S are not P	

  This is a second-order enthymeme. The syllogism is invalid, committing the fallacy of undistributed middle. A universal affirmative minor premise, "All glittering things are precious metals," would make the syllogism valid, but this proposition would be false and would make the argument unsound.

  2. This must be a good book; it was chosen by the Book-of-the-Month Club.

  3. Some of the things alleged by the spiritualists are incredible, because they contradict the laws of nature.

  4. No wristwatch keeps perfect time, for all wristwatches are subject to irregular motions.

  5. The energy crisis, being man-made, can be man-solved.

  6. She is a Phi Beta Kappa, so she must have been a bookworm.

  7. We are on the trail of the criminal, for we have found his footprints.

  8. We need to increase the size and power of our military power, because the Russians are increasing the size of theirs.

9. Only organisms are animals; therefore, this creature is an organism.

10. Only churches have cross-crowned spires; therefore, this building must be a church.

11. "He would not take the crown; therefore 'tis certain he was not ambitious." (*Julius Caesar,* III, ii)

12. This medicine cured my son's cough, so it will therefore cure mine.

13. War is an evil and should be abolished.

14. The speaker criticized free enterprise; he must be a communist.

15. UCLA is raising its standards for admission. That is why we here at USC have to raise ours.

16. None but material bodies gravitate; therefore air is a material body.

17. All romanticists are idealistic. The "New Left" is idealistic. The conclusion is obvious.

18. There must be something wrong with him; look how pale he is.

19. Evidently the patient has a fever, for he keeps asking for water.

20. No one has ever seen a soul; therefore, you cannot know for certain that you have a soul.

21. "He is a leprous man, he is unclean." (Lev. 13)

22. Racial discrimination is never tolerable in American democracy, since it is always unjust.

23. "He that is of God heareth God's words. Ye therefore hear them not."

24. "Death cannot be an evil, being universal." (Goethe)

25. Since this man hates his fellow man, he cannot love God.

26. It is always easier for a rich person to be moral and law-abiding than it is for a poor person, for a rich person does not need to steal bread.

27. Being mortal, do not bear immortal hatred.

28. No man is free, for every man is a slave either to money or to fortune.

29. Not all kind acts are moral, since some altruistic acts are not moral.

30. Nothing intelligible puzzles me, but logic puzzles me.

FIVE

Verbose Arguments

1. DEADWOOD

Our final task is learning how to remove excess verbiage from an argument to clarify its structure. Arguments are often encumbered with wordiness, repetition, and irrelevance. To understand these arguments, it is necessary to eliminate this deadwood from them. Sometimes this simply means ignoring long, drawn-out introductions, as in the following example from Og Mandino's classic salesman's manual, *The Greatest Salesman in the World:*[1]

> Today I will be master of my emotions. The tides advance; the tides recede. Winter goes and summer comes. Summer wanes and the cold increases. The sun rises; the sun sets. The moon is full; the moon is black. The birds arrive; the birds depart. Flowers bloom; flowers fade. Seeds are sown; harvests are reaped. All nature is a circle of moods and I am part of nature and so, like the tides, my moods will rise; my moods will fall. Today I will be master of my emotions.

The point of this argument is the penultimate sentence: "All nature is a circle of moods and I am part of nature and so, like the tides, my moods will rise; my moods will fall." This is a classic example of our syllogism. For purposes of logical evaluation, all the preceding is irrelevant, however poetic or moving it may be.

What applies to lengthy introductions can also apply to conclusions. The following is a typical example:[2]

1. New York: Frederick Fell, 1973, p. 9.
2. Gary H. Snouffer, *Life Insurance Agent* (New York: Arco, 1979), p. ix.

It is important that you study this book thoroughly and with diligence. The state insurance departments which administer insurance examinations take seriously their responsibility to protect the public from unqualified persons. For that reason, life insurance examinations cannot be considered easy to pass. Prospective agents who take their task of studying lightly have been surprised to learn that they have failed examinations. Fortunately, those prospective agents who were qualified undertook study with more earnestness and passed examinations on subsequent occasions. While examinations cannot be considered easy, neither should they be considered unreasonably difficult. The purpose of the examination is to test your knowledge of the type of information contained in this book. If you study thoroughly, you have a good chance of passing.

The last three sentences merely repeat what was said, which, abbreviated, is:

Insurance examinations are not easy to pass without proper preparation. Therefore prepare yourself for them—by buying and reading this book—if you desire to pass them.

Sometimes arguments contain lengthy background material. The background is often helpful but sometimes makes the core argument difficult to pick out. Notice how this applies to the following editorial:

Putting Freedom in Bonds

The city of Palm Springs has a settled policy in renting municipal facilities to private groups. The city requires the purchase of insurance to protect against possible damage to municipal property. The amount of insurance depends on the assessment by the city of the potential risk.

When the Rotary Club rented facilities for an antique sale, the city required the organization to buy $300,000 in insurance. For the Palm Springs Mounted Police Rodeo and Dance, the city required $1 million in insurance.

When the Ku Klux Klan asked for permission to hold a rally in a Civic Center auditorium, the city decided that the potential risk of property damage was high and demanded a $5 million insurance policy from the Klan at a cost of $2,000. The Klan refused and, instead, held a rally on the City Hall steps to protest the insurance requirement.

The Palm Springs regulation is applied without discrimination to all groups, and this evenhandedness poses a problem. A line should be drawn between nonpolitical events and a meeting held expressly for discussion of public issues. A bond requirement for a political meeting imposes an unjustified burden on free speech and violates the First Amendment.

Although the information in the first three paragraphs is helpful and necessary, it is only background to the real argument. This is too much background and overshadows the main argument, which, restated in syllogistic form, amounts to the following:

Bond requirements for political meetings are unjust and violate freedom of speech.
The KKK requested such a meeting.
It was therefore unjust and a violation of its freedom of speech to have required such a bond of it.

Stating the argument so plainly, dislodged from its verbose background, makes its major flaw more apparent. This flaw is that the KKK is not an ordinary type of political organization engaging in ordinary types of political discussion and deliberation. Its type of discussion poses special risks, which the city was trying to protect itself against. Extended passages like this make it difficult to find these flaws, or even the core of the argument.

Can you locate the argument in this story about Josiah Wedgwood? Can you pick out its main flaw?

Josiah Wedgwood was the originator of a most exquisite and beautiful style of pottery. It is exceedingly rare and much admired. He was a man of fine talent and of a princely nature. An English nobleman called upon him once and desired to inspect the potteries. He was shown around the plant by a lad of about fifteen years, while Mr. Wedgwood followed, some steps behind.

The nobleman was a reckless and outspoken man who had no reverence for sacred things and no faith in God, and expressed himself in what would be called "clever" profanity and jested about sacred things. The boy was at first shocked by the nobleman's irreverence, but was soon captured by his cleverness and laughed heartily at the brilliant remarks which he made.

When they returned to the office, the boy was dismissed and Mr. Wedgwood held up before the nobleman a most rare and beautiful vase and described the long process through which it had gone before it was perfected. The visitor held out his hand to receive it, but the artist let it fall on the floor and it was immediately broken to atoms. The nobleman was angry, and said, "I wanted that for my collection." The artist immediately replied: "My Lord, there are other things more precious than this vase which can never be restored. I can make you another piece of pottery equal to, or better, than this, and I will do so, but you can never give back to that boy who has just left us his simple faith and his religious reverence which you have destroyed by making light of sacred things." (H. T. Kerr, *Catholic Quote*)

The main argument was not given until the very end. Restated in syllogistic form, the argument asserts:

Mocking sacred tradition is damaging and corrupting.
You did so.
You are therefore guilty of causing permanent spiritual damage to this young boy.

Unlike the previous argument, the flaw here lies in its major premise, not in its minor. Our reply here might therefore be: Laughing and making light occasionally of sacred things doesn't necessarily mean we will always do so or that it will always lead to serious, corrupting consequences. We have all done this at one time or another without causing permanent damage to ourselves or others.

Can you isolate the argument in the following advertisement? Can you see its main flaw?

What On Earth Makes Kurs Better?

> Kurs goes to the source—nature itself. We use only natural fruits, herbs, seeds, roots and berries in creating each liqueur's taste. But we don't stop there. We search the globe for the absolutely choicest ingredients, wherever they may be grown. Why do we go to such lengths to acquire these ingredients? Simply because the principle that guided Leo Kurs in creating and perfecting each of his liqueurs over four hundred years ago remains as true today as it was then—the best ingredients in the world mean the best-tasting drinks. So the next time you shop for your favorite liqueur, consider the source.

If you are having trouble finding its flaw, try putting the argument in syllogistic form.

2. JARGON

Like wordiness, *jargon* (the use of uncommon words or specialized terms) can also obscure meaning. Here is a typical example of it:

> In any formal organization, the goals as reflected in the system of functional differentiation result in a distinctive pattern of role differentiation. In turn, role differentiation, whether viewed hierarchically or horizontally, leads to what Mannheim called 'perspectivistic thinking,' namely, incumbency in particular status induces a corresponding set of perceptions, attitudes and values.

With diligence, we could dig out the meaning of this passage, but no writer should require this of his or her reader. If this passage is trying to say, "Different people have different jobs, and people in different jobs tend to see and think differently," the writer could say it that way. Pompous and pedantic language may prove unintelligible.

President Franklin D. Roosevelt understood this very well. He was once handed an order issued by the Public Administration Bureau during World War II, which read:

> Such preparation shall be made as will completely obscure all Federal Buildings and nonfederal buildings occupied by the Federal Government during an air-raid for any period of time from visibility by reason of internal or external illumination.

Roosevelt responded: "Tell them that in a building where they have to keep work going, to put something across the windows."

Does this mean we should eliminate or avoid big words? Of course not. But we should always strive to be concise.

Strunk and White, in their classic book *The Elements of Style,* presented this matter in these three sentences:[3]

> Vigorous writing is concise. A sentence should contain no unnecessary words, a paragraph no unnecessary sentences, for the same reason that a drawing should have no unnecessary lines and a machine no unnecessary parts. This requires not that the writer make all his sentences short, or that he avoid all detail and treat his subjects only in outline, but that every word tell.

Writing that conforms to these simple principles is memorable and powerful. Just think of the Lord's Prayer, the Twenty-third Psalm, and Lincoln's Gettysburg Address. These passages aren't totally free of big words, but they are free of bombast and pedantry.

Here are some examples of shorter passages that are simply profound:

Newton: "If I have seen further, it is by standing on the shoulders of giants."

Nietzsche: "Whoever, at any time, has undertaken to build a new heaven has found the strength for it in his own hell."

Old Russian proverb: "Oxen do not move a heavy load with a quick jerk, but with a long, steady pull."

Thoreau: "If a man is out of step with his fellows it may be that he hears a different drummer; let him step to the music which he hears."

St. Francis of Assisi: "God, grant me the serenity to accept the things I cannot change, the courage to change the things I can, and the wisdom to know the difference."

Old saying: He who only hopes is hopeless.

I am sure you can add your own favorite examples that are brief, simple, and clear.

It is not always possible to say things simply or briefly; an author will sometimes need to draw from a larger fund of words. Yet, as the following passage on the nature of wisdom by the American philosopher Brand Blanchard shows, this can be achieved without sacrificing clarity and without needless complication:[4]

> But we have said that the aim of the great philosophers was not merely understanding but also wisdom; and what is that? It is the grasp of the relative values of life, supplemented by practical judgment regarding the means of achieving them. The wise man is the opposite of the fanatic and the hothead, the provincial, the bigot, and the crank. For most men there is a tendency to make mountains, good or ill, out of their own particular molehills; if they are business men, to measure people by

---

3. Third edition. New York: Macmillan, 1978.
4. *Preface to Philosophy* (New York: Macmillan, 1946), Part II: "Personal Ethics," p. 189.

their efficiency and power to make money; if they are musicians, to lose themselves in a world of sound; if they are scientists, to overrate exact knowledge and underrate what is done for us by poetry, art, and religion.

The wise man knows the place of these things in the scheme of life as a whole, and this gives him weight in counsel. He knows that money and possessions are means, not ends. He knows the difference between pleasures of the moment and enduring satisfactions, between being great and being famous, between sex attraction and love, between reverence and superstition, between solidity and show in literature, art, and life. He knows that in the human lot some evils are unavoidable, that loss and disease and old age are bound to come; and he has made his peace with their coming. And so when he is overtaken by these things, he is not overcome by them because he has drawn their sting in advance. He has achieved the serenity of the long view.

At the other extreme is writing of this sort:

Their libidinal impulses being reciprocal, they integrated their individual erotic drives and brought them within the same frame of reference.

Can you see that all this passage is probably saying (for who can be sure) is that "feeling sexually attracted to each other, they had a tryst"?

And what do you think this town ordinance is attempting to communicate to us?

When litter is in the immediate vicinity of an individual and that individual has other property in his immediate possession which is of the same brand name, such person or persons shall be presumed to have caused the litter to be abandoned in the immediate vicinity.

Not so immediately apparent is the meaning of the following passage:

Those who seek to change schools must avoid the assumption that adjusting the balance of attention to the several domains of the school's instructional program is all that need concern them. Our data suggest that the caring way in which the school conducts this educational function is a major factor in determining client satisfaction paralleling in importance perceived attention to intellectual matters in the instructional program.

The big words aren't confusing in this passage; verbosity and needless complexity are. For example, we understand what "seek to change schools" means, but what does "adjusting the balance of attention to the several domains of the school's instructional program" mean? We may understand "Our data suggest that the caring way in which the schools conducts this educational function," but can we say the same of the rest of the sentence? Why "*client* satisfaction"? Does this refer to the students or to their parents? And why "*perceived* attention to intellectual matters"? How is that different from "attention to intellectual matters"?

It is not, then, a matter of avoiding big words, but rather, as Strunk and White point out, of using the right words, words that ''tell,'' as in the following paragraph from John Stuart Mill's Introduction to his famous essay ''On Liberty,'' published in 1859:

> The object of this Essay is to assert one very simple principle as entitled to govern absolutely the dealings of society with the individual in the way of compulsion and control, whether the means used be physical force in the form of legal penalties, or the moral coercion of public opinion. That principle is, that the sole end for which mankind are warranted, individually or collectively, in interfering with the liberty of action of any of their number, is self-protection. That the only purpose for which power can be rightly exercised over any member of a civilized community, against his will, is to prevent harm to others. His own good, either physical or moral, is not a sufficient warrant. He cannot rightfully be compelled to do or forbear because it will be better for him to do so, because it will make him happier, because, in the opinions of others, to do so would be wise or even right. These are good reasons for remonstrating with him or reasoning with him, or persuading him, or entreating him, but not for compelling him, or visiting him with any evil in case he do otherwise. To justify that, the conduct from which it is desired to deter him must be calculated to produce evil to someone else. The only part of the conduct of anyone, for which he is amenable to society, is that which concerns others. In the part which merely concerns himself his independence is, of right, absolute. Over himself, over his own body and mind, the individual is sovereign.

3. EXTENDED ARGUMENTS

Don't confuse verbosity with length. As we noted earlier, some things take more space to express than others.

Notice, for example, how well the following passage from a real-estate investment manual is organized.[5]

> *What's good for real estate is good for the country.*
> The tax benefits that have made real estate the leading shelter investment in the country will not go away. They may be changed, but the changes could be for the better, as in 1981. And, even if they're for the worse, as in 1982, they won't be much worse.
> One thing is certain—they will not be terminal.
> That is because the national economy depends much more on real estate than on any other factor. Consider these benefits of real estate development, rehabilitation or preservation:
>
> - Housing starts not only create jobs and homes, and use great amounts of raw materials, but they also sell home furnishings, appliances, services and even autos. When new home starts are low, all of these related industries and many more are depressed.

5. Jerry C. Davis, *Today's Real Estate Tax Shelters* (Atlanta, Georgia: Hume Publishing Inc., 1985), pp. 3–4.

- Rehabilitation of buildings has spawned many other businesses, and helped improve structures of all types, from houses to shopping centers.

- Commercial and industrial growth depends on a supply of buildings adequate to provide the necessary space for doing business and making products.

- Intelligent tax incentives have helped to preserve some of the finer buildings in the country, and to restore culturally significant buildings that might otherwise have been destroyed.

Any way you look at it, real estate development, rehabilitation and exchange is in the national interest. So much so that even talk of a flat tax, in which everyone pays the same percentage of the cost of running the government, usually includes a caveat to allow some housing deductions. Not to do so would be political suicide in a nation where two-thirds of the population lives in an owned dwelling, and most of the other third would like to.

Notice that the main point is expressed at the very beginning—not, as in the Palm Springs editorial, at the end, almost as an afterthought. It is also underlined to make certain that the reader does not overlook its importance. The writer goes on to explain in clear terms why real estate is indeed a good investment.

Or consider the following "Guidelines on Sexism" from a booklet distributed by Prentice-Hall to their authors to guide them in the preparation of their manuscripts:[6]

Sexism in books includes sins of omission as well as of commission and bias in thought and concept as well as in language. Those who write and edit textbooks need to be particularly sensitive to both areas, for the portrayal of roles and life situations as exclusively masculine or exclusively feminine or the more subtle omission of women as participants in the action is just as much bias as is the general use of *he* or *man* to characterize all human beings. The purpose of establishing guidelines for nonsexist language is to help remove the conceptual and linguistic barriers that now artificially divide many aspects of life and work by gender. They are intended to sensitize both authors and editors to the many ways in which sexism may be expressed and to give them some tools with which to attack the problem.

These guidelines therefore contain "checklists" of things to look for in reading or in editing a manuscript as well as specific kinds of expressions to change or avoid. Eliminating sexism requires as much attention to thought and attitude as it does to pronouns and occupation titles. Much in the same way as one can observe the letter but not the spirit of the law, one can carefully use *he or she* or *they* and yet have a book that in fact ignores women as equal partners in the enterprise of transmitting or expanding human knowledge.

Striking a balance is tricky: women in many cultures and in many eras have been treated as second-class citizens, and certainly the laws and rhetoric of recent years have yet to become part of everyday reality. But to recognize the contributions of women, past and present, is not only to correct the record; it is to make the facts available to those who will create and live out new social realities. And to treat people as human beings, as members of a common group, without identifying them

6. *Prentice-Hall Author's Guide,* 5th ed. (1978).

by gender is to promote changes in attitude that can liberate both men and women and allow society to take advantage of each individual's full potential.

Notice how the main point is stated in the very first sentence, not hidden somewhere in the text to be dug out. Notice, too, how this main point (that sexism can take more than one form) is not dropped but is expanded on in the very next sentence. The rest of the paragraph goes on to assert the value of adopting this new approach and how it might be accomplished. Thus we have here a clear statement of the problem, a reason why we should try to solve it, and a suggestion as to how we might do so.

As these last two examples show, length itself is not objectionable. Although a longer passage requires more attention and concentration on our part, and more time to read, if it is properly organized it can prove challenging rather than frustrating.

If writing is worthwhile, it will contain a piece of reasoning—an argument—that appeals to our understanding and (if justified) commands our assent. The true challenge of such writing for us is to find that core.

See whether you can do so in the following essay from *Time* magazine by Roger Rosenblatt, entitled ''The Baby in the Factory'':[7]

Three weeks ago, the nation recoiled at the story of a microcephalic child, called Baby Doe by the court, who apparently was born without parents. Judy Stiver, the surrogate mother who bore him after being artificially inseminated, claimed that Baby Doe belonged to Alexander Malahoff, who had contracted to pay Stiver $10,000 on delivery. Malahoff, who is separated from his wife, and who hoped the baby might reunite them, accepted the deformed child in the beginning, and had him baptized. Later he rejected the boy, contending Baby Doe was not his own. Last week a blood test proved him right. This established, the Stivers said they were willing to receive the child, thus granting Malahoff his money back, along with an end to a story nobody wanted to hear in the first place, one that, when it was finally played out, involved an array of several unattractive personalities, a multimillion-dollar lawsuit, the specter of baby selling, the suspicion of fraud and deception, and a tasteless denouement on a television talk show, where the M.C. spoke of ''renting a womb.''

But the sleaziness of this particular affair did not account for its disturbing effect on the public. From Baby Doe's birth on Jan. 10, he was seen and discussed as a piece of inferior merchandise, an imperfect creature come into the world as damaged goods. The mother disavowed motherhood; the father said ''Not mine.'' Yet there was the child, frail but present. Deposited on the doorstep, he had to belong to someone.

In a sense, he belonged to everyone for those three weeks, and that universal parenthood may be worth remembering. Baby Doe was the product of a beneficent social impulse. Malahoff wished him into existence, and Stiver provided the incubator, but the context and impetus for the birth were in the public realm, the generally, if warily accepted idea that if infertile people want children strongly enough, then modern science ought to offer a way. Thus arose the recent and remarkable inventions of surrogate parents and test-tube babies. No one is wholly comfortable with these mechanisms, including the principals, but when the baby shows up, glowing and cooing, most reservations dissipate in a hurry. A life has been created, after all, even if it has been done a bit oddly and at various removes.

What happens, on the other hand, when a baby shows up neither glowing nor cooing, but, like Baby Doe, with a strep infection and too small a head, a sign of probable mental retardation? What happens when one is reminded of the numerical odds in such things, when normal reality intrudes on the man-made miracle? It was easy to condemn Stiver for feeling no motherly connection to the child, yet surrogate motherhood necessarily precluded those feelings, indeed made reasonable her self-imposed detachment. It was easy, too, to be appalled by Malahoff's rejection, but the baby he originally ordered up was to be his own, not another father's. Oh yes, there was the matter of the deformity, which cried out for special kindness and scruples, so one might think that Stiver or Malahoff would have been willing to take Baby Doe, no matter what. But who would not hesitate before deciding to accept a retarded child if one really had the choice? And the circumstances did present a choice.

Choice may, in fact, be the key to the matter, the center of public uneasiness. On the face of it, or even in the heart of it, there is nothing wrong with the idea of surrogate parenthood, or with any indirect process by which a child is created because somebody wants him. The essential difference between such a procedure and an opposite one like abortion is that in the surrogate situation someone does want the child, the desire being compelling. Indeed, everyone concerned wants the child; the prospective family and the surrogate parent too, either for profit or as an act of philanthropy. It may be argued that adoption is a cleaner and less cumbersome method, for all its bureaucratic impediments, but this is not an issue enhanced by taking sides. A couple wants a child. If the insemination is artificial, the parental attitude is real.

The disturbing element here, however, the one this story exposed to the air, is the implication that these processes, which satisfy that basic human desire and which do so by manipulating a basic human act, are merely mechanical, technologically clever, new testaments to American know-how. Pregnant women often joke gently about their offspring ''in the oven,'' but in a jokeless context, where the baby in question is being cooked up on consignment, there is cause for real worry. With all the potential joys of scientifically created parenthood, the last thing one wishes to encourage is the impersonal approach. What is being cooked up in each instance is not a cake or a car or a mail-order watch. It is a person, small-headed or not, and any situation that suggests otherwise is not just dismaying but dangerous.

In the case of Stiver-Malahoff we observed a problem fairly simple to resolve. Malahoff has been taken out of the picture, and the Stivers now claim to be ready to accept their responsibilities. But the problem between Malahoff and themselves would never have arisen had Baby Doe arrived healthy. How far was this matter from a slightly different one in which some future Malahoff, while being proved the true father of an imperfect boy, decides nonetheless that a microcephalic baby was not what he had in mind? He would like to send it back, demand a refund. The law might stand in his way, of course, but the heart of the issue is not legal. A procedure has been devised in which a human being is literally conceived as a manufactured product. Therefore, consciously or not, all the participants in that procedure tend to regard the product either as the flower of a growth industry or, if a flaw appears, as industrial waste.

This is probably why the story was so troubling, and why it ought to be. What we were viewing was not a mishap in a procedure to be condemned or abhorred, or even regulated with excruciating detail—though regulations will help—but rather something new and fragile, like a baby, to be watched with great and serious care. Technological parenthood may have the trappings of a business, but it is not a business; it is the answer to someone's most personal prayers. So it should be seen and handled. If the answer to a particular prayer happens to emerge deformed, it is no less the prayer's answer; and, as many parents of such "damaged goods" have discovered, they sometimes give more contentment to a family than whole and healthy children and thus provide answers to different prayers entirely.

The point is simply that these goods are people, however they may be produced. Nor is any child to be judged or treated as a factory reject merely because something is wrong with him. One forgets these things from time to time, lost in pride at our advancement.

This is obviously a more difficult piece of writing. The author doesn't state his main point in the first sentence, which might have made it easier for us. In this respect it may seem a lot like the Palm Springs editorial, but it isn't. If you have perhaps four short paragraphs in which to make a point, then each paragraph must count. You cannot afford to devote three of those four to background and only the last one to your basic argument. When you have more space, you can be more expansive, approach your theme from more than one perspective, and paint the background in greater detail. But there is always the risk that this detail and expansiveness will overwhelm your main argument.

Do you think this is the case with this essay? If not, why not? And what is its main thesis? Is it possible to express it with the following syllogism?

All babies are human beings "ordered up by someone."
All human beings "ordered up by someone" are beings who must be cared for by those who have "ordered them up," regardless of what they get.
All babies are beings who must be cared for by those who have "ordered them up," regardless of what they get.

It is important to apply this technique to extended arguments. Only then can we be sure we have understood the passage or argument, and know how to evaluate and respond to it.

SUMMARY

Arguments are often encumbered with repetition, verbosity, and irrelevance. To get to the heart of these arguments we must remove such verbiage. Doing so may involve ignoring longwinded introductions or conclusions. Where the argument is verbose throughout, other types of editing may be required, as in the case of arguments using jargon.

Jargon is the use of uncommon words or specialized terms to express something that can be stated more directly. To understand arguments filled with jargon, we must simplify the language and structure, eliminate unnecessary words and expressions, or substitute other, more familiar words for the inflated and pretentious ones.

Don't confuse wordiness with length. Some things require more space to express. Extended arguments demand more of our attention and take longer to master; often, however, they repay our time and effort with new insight into the problems they confront.

--- **Exercises** ---

I. DIRECTIONS: Rewrite the following passages as concisely as possible, clarifying their meaning and, as far as possible, putting each into syllogistic form. (See answers in appendix.)

1. Surely also there is something strange in representing the man of perfect blessedness as a solitary or a recluse. Nobody would deliberately choose to have all the good things in the world, if there was a condition that he was to have them all by himself. Man is a social animal, and the need for company is in his blood. Therefore the happy man must have company, for he has everything that is naturally good, and it will not be denied that it is better to associate with friends than with strangers, with men of virtue than with the ordinary run of persons. We conclude then that the happy man needs friends. (Aristotle, *Ethics*)

2. **Mother Nature is Lucky Her Products Don't Need Labels**

    [Ad shows a picture of a hand holding a fresh orange]

    All foods, even natural ones, are made up of chemicals. But natural foods don't have to list their ingredients. So it's often assumed they're chemical-free. In fact, the ordinary orange is a miniature chemical factory. And the good old potato contains arsenic among its more than 150 ingredients. This doesn't mean natural foods are dangerous. If they were, they wouldn't be on the market. The same is true of man-made foods. All man-made foods are tested for safety. And they often provide more nutrition, at a lower cost, than natural foods. They even use many of the same chemical ingredients. So you see, there really isn't much difference between foods made by Mother Nature and those made by man. What's artificial is the line drawn between them.

    Monsanto . . . Without Chemicals Life Itself Would Be Impossible

3. The day *may* come when the rest of the animal creation may acquire those rights which never could have been withholden from them but by the hand of tyranny. The French have already discovered that the black-

ness of the skin is no reason why a human being should be abandoned without redress to the caprice of a tormentor. It may one day come to be recognized that the number of the legs, the villosity of the skin, or the termination of the *os sacrum* are reasons equally insufficient for abandoning a sensitive being to the same fate. What else is it that should trace the insuperable line? Is it the faculty of reason, or perhaps the faculty of discourse? But a full-grown horse or dog is beyond comparison a more rational, as well as a more conversable animal, than an infant of a day, or a week, or even a month, old. But suppose they were otherwise, what would it avail? The question is not, Can they *reason*? nor Can they *talk*? but, Can they *suffer*? (Jeremy Bentham, *The Principles of Morals and Legislation,* 1789)

4. Your Editor made some unfortunate and unjustified criticisms concerning the newly established Palau Postal Service. He wrote: "With a population of 12,000, the island has its own postal system. That brings up two questions: how many "entities" with a population of 12,000 or less maintain their own postal systems? What if each U.S. city with 12,000 or more residents had its own postal system?"
   How many entities of 12,000 or less maintain their own postal system? I am sure that the names of Aitutaki, Ascension, the Australian Antarctic Territory, the British Antarctic Territory, Cocos (Keeling) Islands, the Falkland Islands, the Falkland Islands Dependencies, Nauru, Nevis, Norfolk, Penrhyn, Pitcairn Islands, Ross Dependency, St. Helena, Tristan da Cunha, Tokelau Islands, Tuvalu, (British) Virgin Islands, and Zil Elwagne Sesel (formerly British Indian Ocean Territory), must ring a bell with most philatelists. Most of these "entities" do not have populations even approaching the 5,000 mark.
   One case in point is that of the Falklands, which before the outbreak of war between Britain and Argentina had a civilian population hovering just below the 2,000 mark. Not only has the tiny British outpost issued stamps for more than a century, but hundreds of soldiers died in the recent fight for control of that "entity." (*American Philatelist,* June 1983, p. 492)

5.   **Come With Old Khayyam**

Oh, come with old Khayyam, and leave the Wise
To talk; one thing is certain, that life flies;
    One thing is certain, and the Rest is Lies;
The flower that once has blown for ever dies.

Ah, make the most of what we yet may spend,
Before we too into the Dust Descend;
    Dust into Dust, and under Dust, to lie,
Sans Wine, Sans Song, sans Singer and
            sans End!

                          —Omar the Tentmaker

6. "Nothing in the world—indeed nothing even beyond the world—can possibly be conceived which could be called good without qualification except a *good will.* Intelligence, wit, judgment, and the other talents of the mind, however they may be named, or courage, resoluteness, and perseverance as qualities of temperament, are doubtless in many respects good and desirable. But they can become extremely bad and harmful if the will, which is to make use of these gifts of nature and which in its special constitution is called character, is not good. It is the same with the gifts of fortune. Power, riches, honor, even health, general well-being, and the contentment with one's condition which is called happiness, make for pride and even arrogance if there is not a good will to correct their influence on the mind and on its principles of action so as to make it universally conformable to its end. It need hardly be mentioned that the sight of a being adorned with no feature of a pure and good will, yet enjoying uninterrupted prosperity, can never give pleasure to a rational impartial observer. Thus the good will seems to constitute the indispensable condition even of worthiness to be happy." (Kant, *Foundations of the Metaphysics of Morals*)

II. DIRECTIONS: Which one of the two following translations of a passage from Plato's *Protagoras* do you prefer? Explain your choice.

The auditors of such a debate ought to be impartial but not neutral in their sentiments. They should listen to both impartially but take the part of the wiser, not the worse. And I implore you, Socrates and Protagoras, to make mutual concessions and to contravene but not to controvert. For contravention is the argumentation of friends, but controversy is the disputation of opponents. Thus will you, the speakers, receive approbation but not acclamation from us, since approbation is the critical judgment of the mind, while acclamation may be the hypocritical flattery of the tongue. And we, your hearers, will enjoy gratification, not delectation, for gratification is the mind's delight in learning and delectation is the body's pleasure in eating. (translated by Paul Shorey[8])

You are quite right, Critias. Those who are present at discussions of this kind must divide their attention between the speakers impartially, but not equally. The two things are not the same. They must hear both alike, but not give equal weight to each. More should be given to the wiser, and less to the other. I add my plea, Protagoras and Socrates, that you should be reconciled. Let your conversation be a discussion not a dispute. A discussion is carried on among friends with goodwill, but a dispute is between rivals and enemies. In this way our meeting will be best conducted. You, the speakers, will be esteemed by us—esteemed, I say, not praised, for esteem is a genuine feeling in the hearts of the audience, whereas praise is often on the lips of men belying their true conviction—and we who listen will experience enjoyment rather than

8. *What Plato Said* (Chicago: University of Chicago Press, 1973), p. 127.

pleasure. Enjoyment can result from learning and partaking in the intellectual activity of the mind alone, but pleasure arises rather from eating or other forms of physical indulgence. (translated by W. K. C. Guthrie[9])

III. DIRECTIONS: Abbreviate the following three passages and state the thesis of each. Try to express their main arguments in syllogistic form.

1.   **If Fair's Fair, End the "Windfall Profit" Tax[10]**

Several politicians and the commentators who mirror their views have decried in recent days the fact that the Administration's plan for tax reform modifies but doesn't eliminate the current tax treatment for what are called "intangible drilling costs." They view this—with alarm, of course—as evidence of "buckling" to the oil industry, and they decry the "unfairness" of this treatment.

Well, let's take a moment to see what "intangible drilling costs" really are. And while we're at it, let's look as well at the overall question of which taxes are fair and which aren't. (We'll skip the issue of tax simplification. We'll merely note that within hours after it was announced, the Treasury issued a 461-page book to explain its latest plan.)

Intangible drilling costs are the costs of preparing and drilling oil, gas and geothermal wells that do not involve the purchase of tangible property. They include the amounts paid for labor, fuel, supplies, and technical services. They also include site-preparation costs, which are considerable in those instances when man-made islands from which to drill have to be built, or canals dredged so rigs can be brought to the well sites. These are among the costs that taxpayers may choose to treat as either a business expense or a capital item on their tax returns. Expenses may be written off the year they are incurred; the cost of capitalized items may be depreciated over their useful lives.

Under the new tax plan, the option to expense eighty percent of intangible drilling costs would be retained, with certain technical restrictions. The survival of the option is what has given rise to the cries of unfairness.

We wonder why the cry has been raised at all—unless it's because those who raise it still regard the oil companies as convenient whipping boys. If the money spent on intangible drilling costs—for items which have no salvage value—had to be capitalized and couldn't be recovered promptly, the companies would have a diminished amount of cash available to find and develop new secure supplies of oil and gas. And America would become more dependent on foreign energy sources. But too few ask the hard questions about the nation's future oil and gas supplies. Other questions also go unasked.

What is the difference, for example, between research and develop-

---

9. Plato, *Protagoras and Meno* (Harmondsworth, England: Penguin, 1982), pp. 70–71.

10. © Mobil Corporation. Reprinted with permission of Mobil Corporation.

ment expenditures for new and improved products, which will be marketed for many years in the future, and the intangible costs associated with drilling an oil or gas well that should produce for several years? What is the difference between intangible drilling costs and the advertising expenses to promote the sale of such products well into the future? To us, the answer seems clear: There is no difference. Even so, has anyone claimed that the 100 percent expensing of these items (versus 80 percent for oil and gas) is a tax break? We doubt it.

But we wonder most of all why politicians and commentators remain strangely silent about the continuing existence of the so-called "windfall profit" tax, imposed *only* on the oil industry back in 1980. Industry profits have been trending down since, and if "fairness" is to be the new litmus test of tax policy, how can the government tax "windfalls" that don't exist?

The "windfall profit" tax was never more than a punitive measure, unrelated to profitability. It was—and is—a tax on production. Since it is applied to oil that hasn't even been discovered yet, it's clearly unrelated to the cost of such oil.

Those who claim the new tax plan unfairly favors oil can easily prove their newfound dedication to the principle of equity. Let them repeal the "windfall profit" tax in the interest of fairness, and leave the tax structure alone where it clearly already meets the fairness test.

2.   **Krishna Consciousness and Religious Freedom**[11]

I've asked myself in recent weeks, as there has been more and more controversy about the Hare Krishna movement (many devotees of which I've personally known and respected highly), "Why is it that suddenly this movement has come in for such attention, to the point that one might even begin to speak of harassment? Why is this?" And I have to confess now, as a theologian mainly committed to Christianity, that I think it indicates a feeling of guilt and a feeling of failure on the part of those who have tried to preserve something of the critical and creative spiritual possibilities that Christianity itself offers.

Could it be that we have allowed Christianity itself and perhaps Judaism to be so identified with the values of accumulation, profit, performance, success, and material gain—which are, after all, the main values of our society—that it takes something as apparently esoteric and exotic as a movement coming from India to remind us that there is in fact another way of life, that there is a way of life that is not built on accumulating profit, property, success, and degrees, but has at its core a certain kind of simplicity and plainness of living, if you will? . . .

Why is it, I asked myself, that we can't hear the voices of prophets from our own tradition, and yet somehow people from as far away as India can bring a message which in some ways sounds so similar?

11. Reprinted by permission of author.

Maybe this is a way that we are being called back to something more essential in our own tradition—a way that God has of reminding us of what we've left behind and forgotten and ignored.

What is the meaning for us of this movement's coming into our midst in this century? I would put it in a very theological sense: What is God saying to us? What does it mean? . . . Are we uncomfortable with this movement because at a certain level we're very uncomfortable with ourselves, with the kind of materialistic society we've built? (Harvey Cox, in a speech at the Center for the Study of World Religions, Harvard University, Nov. 22, 1976)

3.   **The Morals of Remembering**[12]

The style of monuments in Washington (the Lincoln, the Washington, the Jefferson) runs to idealizations in cool, white stone. The places are abstracted: alabaster, clean, undimmed by human tears. They are also shrines for the tourists who come in double-knits and halters. They are entirely American.

A new memorial in Washington will be different. It will be installed on the edge of the Mall, not far from the Washington Monument. It will be utterly European. It will reek of a European suffering and evil.

The memorial, a museum commemorating the millions of Jews and others who died at Auschwitz and Dachau and Treblinka, will be housed in two large, red brick turn-of-the-century buildings. The catastrophic drama of genocide will thus be installed in the middle of the Washington tourist round, along with the Capitol and the cherry blossoms. The museum will detain tourists as the Ancient Mariner seized the wedding guests to make them listen to an uglier tale than they might want to hear.

The idea of such a place has caused a certain subdued muttering. The muttering grants the enormity of the Holocaust, but it suggests: Why should the U.S. Government set aside land and buildings to commemorate a tragedy that occurred on another continent, a horror in which Americans had no part either as victims or persecutors. Americans have their own native horrors. Why not a memorial museum to black slavery? Why not a memorial to the American Indian culture? The American conscience could be engaged much closer to home than Auschwitz.

So says the muttering. But there is a deeper question. It involves a difficult, sometimes grotesque moral calculus of comparative genocides. What does the historical memory remember? Over which slaughters does it grieve? Over which does it pass obliviously? And why?

Consider one that has almost got lost. This is the 50th anniversary of the enforced famine, engineered by Stalin, in which some 8 million to 10 million Ukrainians and Cossacks perished. Their extermination was a matter of state policy, just as the ovens of Dachau were a matter of state policy. The Ukrainian kulaks died under the great brute wheel of an idea. They died for the convenience of the state, to help with the organization of the new order of things.

They died, and yet the grass has grown over the world's memory of their murder. Why? The numbers of the dead would surely qualify that entry (one thinks mordantly) for some genocidal hall of fame. Perhaps that is the sort of museum we need on the edge of the Mall: a home for all the great blood scandals: the Armenians slaughtered by the Turks, the Hutus slain by the Tutsis in Burundi, the Cambodians who have died in Pol Pot's haunting imitation of Stalin's barbarisms.

Is it evil to forget? Is it necessary to remember? Perhaps remembrance is a matter of sociobiology. Perhaps we remember what it is necessary to remember for survival, and we forget what it is necessary to forget. The author Elie Wiesel, a survivor of Auschwitz and Buchenwald, states the case on eloquently pragmatic grounds: "Memory is our shield, our only shield." To Wiesel, only memory can immunize mankind against a repetition of the slaughter.

A memorial, of course, is not the same as a memory. In some deep ways, the two are opposite. The memorial makes memory objective. The memorial rescues suffering from its degrading pointlessness and installs it in the stone or in the photo exhibits and libraries. It is an event in the process of mourning, helping to set the pain to rest at an endurable distance. It helps to heal. It is the thing we build to signal our acceptance. In a way, we make memorials so that we can begin at last to forget. The Holocaust, on that corner of the Mall, must become in some sense something else, something like Wordsworth in paraphrase: horror recollected in tranquility.

A memorial can relieve the poor daily mind of the responsibility of obsessive remembering. Memorials may sometimes simultaneously idealize and trivialize terrible events. On the other hand, one cannot approach the memorial at Hiroshima without seeing and feeling again the apocalyptic flash. Busloads of Japanese children arrive every day and gravely absorb the meaning of the place.

Still, a memorial is a way of saying goodbye. Every memorial needs its proper time. In that sense, American blacks may not yet be ready for a memorial. Slavery, or its long, tenacious afterlife, is still in business. What one sees in Harlem or Watts or South Side Chicago is really slavery in other forms. So it is not yet time for that memorial. Americans still do not know the outcome of slavery. A memorial needs finality. A memorial, the final seal upon the wound and the grief, cannot be articulate until the drama is ended.

Life eventually rejects too many claims being made upon it by the dead. The capacity for grief is finite. Life likes to forget a little. The living, if they are sane, want memory and death and obsession to observe certain house rules. That is difficult in a century in which genocide has become, so to speak, a way of life. It is difficult for great cataclysms to coexist morally with the smaller homely business of things.

At the most obvious, the moral intention of a memorial is simple: Lest we forget. The stone formalizes a relationship between past and future. It solemnizes and legitimizes and dignifies those who have departed into the squalid indignity of death, departed in a way so inhuman that humanity wants to pile on posthumous kindnesses, posthumous significances.

Perhaps it is grotesque for people to wish to commemorate their blackest acts, their atrocities. In their traditional function, memorials glorify our heroes, our battles, our ideals, our (presumably) higher values. Erecting memorials to our horrors is the moral equivalent of impaling heads on spikes by the roadside: it rivets the attention of the passers-by and leaves them with a memorable warning. It is a form of tutoring in the truth, both edifying and horrifying, that man is capable of anything. He can go either way, and does.

Only the faculty of moral memory can begin to redeem the worst deeds. In another context, the poet Robert Lowell wrote: "My eyes have seen what my hand did." Self-awareness is precisely what makes us human, the action of the judging inner eye, the intelligent witness that keeps house in the brain. Memory is eventually a moralist, and memory educates the beast. (Lance Morrow, *Time,* May 23, 1983)

Answers to Selected Exercises

CHAPTER ONE

Exercise I:

1. true; false
2. sentences
3. to be
4. quantifiers
5. hypothetical; disjunctive
6. universal affirmative; universal negative; particular affirmative; particular negative
7. all; some
8. affirmative; negative
9. A, E, I, O
10. rephrased
11. "persons who"; "things that"
12. "all"; "no"
13. universal
14. O
15. I; O
16. reversing; negating

Exercise II:

18. E
20. I

22. O
23. A
26. A
28. E
30. O
31. I

CHAPTER TWO

Exercise III:

15. obverse
16. converse
17. contradictory
18. contrary
19. superimplicate
20. contrapositive
21. contrary
22. obverse
23. superimplicate
24. converse
25. contradictory
26. subimplicate

27. converse
28. obverse
29. subcontrary
30. contradictory
31. obverse
32. contrary
33. contradictory
34. subimplicate

Exercise V:

36. converse
37. contraries
38. subcontraries
39. obverse
40. converse
41. contradictories
42. subimplicate
43. superimplicate
44. obverse
45. contrapositive

CHAPTER THREE

Exercise I:

1. two negatives
2. negative premise, no negative conclusion
3. two negative premises
4. two particular premises
5. negative conclusion, no negative premise
6. illicit minor

Exercise II:

7. I
8. O
9. A
10. E
11. O

Exercise IV:

19. Main difficulty: "Few . . ."
21. Main difficulty: "All . . . are not . . ."

22. Main difficulty: "Only . . ."
23. Main difficulty: "None but . . ."
24. four terms
26. equivocation
28. Main difficulty: "It is false that . . ."
29. Main difficulty: "It is not the case that . . ."
32. four terms
39. Requires obversion.
40. Requires contraposition.
44. four terms
50. Requires contraposition and obversion.

CHAPTER FOUR

Exercise I:

2. first-order
3. first-order
4. first-order
5. third-order
6. first-order
7. first-order
8. first-order
9. second-order
10. second-order
11. first-order
12. first-order
13. first-order
14. first-order
15. first-order
16. second-order
17. third-order
18. first-order
19. first-order
20. first order
21. first-order
22. first-order
23. second-order
24. first-order
25. first-order
26. first-order
27. first-order
28. first-order

29. second-order
30. third-order

CHAPTER FIVE

Exercise I:

1. Man is a social animal and needs the company of other men to be happy.
   The company of friends is better than that of strangers.
   To be happy man needs friends.

3. Animals are similar to humans in being sensitive creatures, susceptible to suffering.
   This is a crucial similarity.
   Basic rights enjoyed by humans should therefore not be denied to them.

5. Life passes one by very quickly into an endless death.
   Make the most, therefore, of what is yet left.

6. Intelligence, wit, judgment, courage, etc., are good but not without qualification.
   They can become bad if combined with a bad will.
   This leaves only a good will itself as the only good thing without qualification in the world.

Index